CREATING A THINKING ORGANIZATION

TO MARTIN AND ROBERT, MY LITTLE ANGELS

CREATING A THINKING ORGANIZATION

Groundrules for Success

Rikki Hunt

with

Tony Buzan

Illustrations by Janet Tapsell

Gower

Published by
Gower Publishing Limited
Gower House
Croft Road
Aldershot
Hampshire GU11 3HR
England

Gower
Old Post Road
Brookfield
Vermont 05036
USA

J.R. Hunt and Tony Buzan have asserted their right under the Copyright, Designs and Patents Act 1988 to be identified as the authors of this work.

Mind Maps® Registered Trade Mark Buzan Organization Ltd.

British Library Cataloguing in Publication Data
Hunt, Rikki
Creating a thinking organization
1. Organizational behaviour 2. Executive ability
I. Title II. Buzan, Tony III. Tapsell, Janet
658.4

ISBN 0 566 08230 6

Library of Congress Cataloging-in-Publication Data
Hunt, Rikki.
Creating a thinking organization / Rikki Hunt with Tony Buzan;
illustrations by Janet Tapsell.
p. cm.
Includes index.
ISBN 0-566-08230-6 (hbk)
1. Organizational effectiveness. 2. Organizational behavior.
3. Organizational change. 4. Management—Decision making.
5. Creative ability in business. I. Buzan, Tony. II. Title.
HD58.9.H86 1999
658.4'06—dc21   99-26292
CIP

Typeset in Garamond Light by Bournemouth Colour Press, Parkstone and printed in Great Britain at the University Press, Cambridge.

CONTENTS

PREFACE

❖

Business has never been as challenging as it is today. We live in an environment in which anyone can set up a company which learns from others' mistakes, copies their ideas and reduces the original company's opportunities.

The evolution into today's business environment can be likened to that of comedy. At the beginning of the twentieth century the music hall comedians travelled round the country with a single set of jokes and routines, making a good living – until, the advent of radio when, suddenly, these jokes could be heard by thousands of people, in different places, at the same time. Then came television, which meant that they could be seen as well as heard. Goodbye music hall tradition. ... A new breed of comedians emerged and most of the music hall comedians faded into obscurity except for a few who, although fragile in health, are still around today. The survival of these few can be attributed to one factor alone – their ability to adapt to their changed environment.

It is said that the top companies of the next millennium have probably not yet been born. That may be true, but it does not have to be. They can be created from the companies of today. Old companies can become new companies, but only if they understand what prevents their transformation.

'We've always done it this way', 'It worked in the past,' 'I don't see the point in changing', 'What's the problem?' are phrases that we've all heard. It is also said that 'You never hear the bullet that kills you' and, likewise, most companies are oblivious to the problem which will cripple them and which is often blindingly obvious to outsiders.

Tomorrow's world *will* be different so we must think about what that means and what to do about it. The current buzz word in organizations is 'intellectual capital', but we must work to achieve a return on this resource just as we do with financial capital. The 'Thinking Organization', as its name implies, uses its intellectual capital as an unfair advantage over those that do not.

In August 1997 the world's first 'Mind Sports Olympiad' took place at the Royal Festival Hall in London. Jan Carendi of Scandia summarized the way forward in his opening address. Here is an extract from that address, which was a powerful 'Call to brains':

> We know that stretched body muscles can take more strain. Likewise we know that stretched minds mean more brain A stretched brain will never return to its original size. Money can be borrowed, processes can be copied, brainpower evades trapping. An original is always better than a good copy. Uniqueness is priceless. Being yourself and stretching your mind is like a stellar explosion. Nobody knows the limits.
>
> While brainpower evades trapping, the results of good thinking can be shared. If you give me a £ sterling and I give you one then we both have one each. But if you give me an idea and I give you another we both have two each.
>
> As I see it, the leadership challenge [of the twenty-first century] is to unleash human potential. Its said that only about 20% of employees' potential is regularly used by employers. Let's assume that we manage to create an environment in which usage is increased to 30% – that is, a 50% increase!
>
> The true value of an organisation is much more than its financial results. It is not only to make money but to make sense and meaning. The true importance of Intellectual Capital is that it is like running at the top of your ability and then accelerating!
>
> So let's stretch our minds. We cannot afford not to do it. It makes dollars and sense.

The winning companies will be those that mobilize the most brains in their companies. This will take courage on the part of those facilitating that mobilization because a direct result of 'switching brains on' will be the questions arising from those brains. They will question anything and everything.

My son, Robert, is four years old and although I think he is the world's most handsome, lively, intelligent and funny four-year-old, I am sure he is no different from other boys of his age. Nevertheless Robert is a 'growing brain', constantly asking 'why'. My answers, I know, will help shape his future.

The 'why?' question is the most basic link between 'old' or 'static' thinking and constant growth so, to facilitate the change in thinking needed in organizations, we must:

O   create a culture which not only allows, but encourages questioning, by everyone, as a matter of course

O   teach thinking in the form of thinking techniques and encourage their constant use.

Many brains have been asleep for some time. When we wake them we need to teach their custodians how to use them in a way which benefits both the individual and business.

Creating a Thinking Organization is concerned with these areas. It presents a practitioner's view of how to run a company or, perhaps more accurately, how to get a company to run itself. It is also the outcome of my own personal journey, reflecting my experiences with a wide variety of companies in terms of size, industry sector and product.

This book will benefit:

O anyone who wants a better lifestyle
O those wanting to achieve more in their chosen career
O principal executives, senior executives and key operating executives looking for a better and more practical way of:
  – unlocking the potential of the people in their organizations
  – finding better working practices for themselves
  – using models to explain both leadership and where the specialist knowledge does, and should, reside in a hierarchy
  – motivating a diverse group of people
O those teaching others, whether academically or socially (for example, youth leaders and the like) and who need 'real world' ways of making their points.

Although this book is written with a business slant, it also provides individual readers with many insights which will allow them to see themselves or others more clearly and show them how to create a personal plan to become more motivated, focused and effective, both inside and outside the work environment.

In the Groundrules parents will find an up-to-date framework which allows them to empower children to take ownership of their actions, to give and receive feedback without feeling threatened and which acts as a modern 'moral code'.

Everyone on the planet is a leader, in the sense that we lead ourselves through a dynamically changing environment. This book will make the difference between being placed in a position of leadership and actually being **a leader who wins – a 'meta leader'.**

> *The combination of a **new culture or environment** and the teaching of **thinking techniques** is stunningly dynamic and is the missing link between understanding the technical side of a business and making the business **win, continuously**.*

The Thinking Organization method works because it deals with the organization as a whole. Without a holistic approach you cannot hope to achieve a whole solution. What you have instead is fad management – which amounts to trying to mend a leaking reservoir with sticking plaster. There is no such thing as a 'quick fix'. Although individuals may be able to change their thinking overnight, translating this into collective actions in the workplace takes time.

This is why short-term fads don't work. With fad management, if you're lucky, you achieve some movement in some people as long as the person driving the fad is still there and the programme is live. But this soon fizzles out when the programme is perceived as being completed.

An example of this would be a 'customer service programme', which requires front-end employees to wear badges with smiling faces. When you end the programme and your staff remove their badges you convey the message 'now we don't have to smile'.

The good news is that by implementing the Thinking Organization process described in this book – essentially putting in the Groundrules and supplementing these with thinking techniques – most of the management concepts with which you are familiar happen anyway. However, they occur as natural **outcomes** rather than forced **inputs**, destined to fail. As you will discover, the **Thinking Organization is not a programme, but a way of life**.

THE BOOK

The book contains four Parts, each of which builds on the one before. The final Part incorporates a detailed implementation plan.

Part I, 'Creating The Environment', is the foundation. It contains the fundamental tools needed to create the environment for a Thinking Organization to emerge. In such an organization thinking and all that results from it (creativity, improved decision-making, personal accountability and so on) become the norm.

These fundamental tools are your vision and mission, which should be memorable, and the Groundrules which are a way of defining and managing every individual relationship.

Part II, 'Thinking in the Environment', builds on Part I by introducing the whole concept of 'thinking' and distinguishing it from 'learning'. It examines how to develop our 'thinking machine' – the brain – and demonstrates, with practical case studies and examples, the power of using thinking techniques.

Part III, 'Leading in the Environment', adds a further dimension by explaining some of the organizational and individual implications of creating a thinking organization. It looks at leadership, using a new Powerbase model, at change and at how to manage the way others see us. It also challenges you, through using a new knowledge model, to question where the 'specialist knowledge base' in any organization is located and where it should be.

Part IV, 'The Thinking Organization in Practice', completes the book with an example of a typical implementation plan, provides some evidence demonstrating the longevity of a Thinking Organization and ends with a complete action plan.

At the end of each Part is a summary of its content, an action plan and a review by Tony Buzan. Throughout the book certain types of material have been identified by the following symbols:

 Overview

 Burmah Petroleum Fuels Ltd. 'story'

 Stories

 Key points

Exercise/example

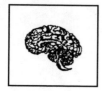

Action

Reviews

These symbols allow you to dip in and out for the reference points most relevant to you.

Whilst the Thinking Organization concept and the Groundrules© belong to Rikki, just as Mind Mapping® belongs to Tony, this book represents the integration of both sets of ideas, based on common beliefs.

I hope that when you have read this book you will believe that you have been given the Groundrules for success!

Rikki Hunt

ACKNOWLEDGEMENTS

Thanks are due to David Simmons, an independent consultant, and Janet Tapsell, Personnel Director for Burmah Petroleum Fuels Ltd, for helping me over a long period to articulate my ideas.

Thanks are also due to all those too numerous to list who completed the questionnaires and are living the Groundrules.

Thanks to Bob Garret (author of *The Fish Rots From The Head*), John Harper, former Professional Development Director of the Institute of Directors, Vanda North, Managing Director of Buzan Centres and my sister Vivienne, all of whom read and commented on early drafts of this book.

A special thank you goes to my son, Martin, who not only contributed the picture used to demonstrate improvement, but also for coming up with the name of my company, Petrol Express.

And, finally, more thanks than I could give in a lifetime to my friend and co-author, Tony Buzan, who not only inspired me with his own thoughts and concepts but also convinced me to write this book, and then held my hand through the complete process, and achieved a perfect balance between criticism and encouragement. I could not have produced this without you, and I will be eternally grateful.

RH

INTRODUCING THE AUTHORS

reating a Thinking Organization is written solely with the practitioner in mind. For someone to want, and be able, to pass on knowledge or ideas, they must have experienced what they profess to teach. Without this experience, ideas and knowledge are theoretical – rather like saying you can drive after reading the *Highway Code* or a mechanics guide. In theory you will understand the process but, unless you have also experienced stalling, skidding, reversing and so on and know what it feels like, then you are not a real driver.

This is especially the case when it comes to the management of organizations. No amount of reading about 'people management' can prepare you for the first time you have to dismiss someone or for the sense of achievement you feel when someone you have recruited becomes a 'star'.

As a practitioner's guide, therefore, this book is inevitably an articulation of personal experience. Although it does not set out to be autobiographical in a formal sense, it does include some of the experiences which led to the ideas described. Some of these may seem very far removed from your own world. The point is, however, not to compare or think 'I'd never do that' or 'I could never do that'. Experiences and future personal goals are individual to each one of us. Mine are included to illustrate the points that emerge during the book. The most fundamental of these is that you can always do more than you think you can.

The book is not about who you are now – it is about who you want to be.

RIKKI HUNT

Just after Easter 1968, after a conversation with a teacher unimpressed by a particular aspect of my behaviour, I made the momentous decision to leave full-time education and find a job.

My older brother Glen, who was critical of my decision, decided to look at my options. As he saw it, I had three:

1   I could concentrate on football – my greatest passion – although my abilities were only average.
2   I could go into TV. After all, he argued, I had the raw material – I was a clown!
3   I could take a job in food retailing. According to Glen, even a nobody could become important in this field and, no matter what happened, everyone would always have to eat! Furthermore, with a Saturday job on Kirkby market, I also had one foot in the door.

So, off I went and found a job with Edward Winston Porter on his market stalls

I learnt a great deal in my first job. On the positive side I discovered that I was not stupid – which was the message I'd received at school. This realization dawned when the UK changed to decimal currency: I found it easy to convert pounds, shillings and pence to new pounds and pence. I also met some wonderful people who I still think of today.

On the negative side I felt taunted by my employer. It was, and still is, common practice to play practical jokes on those who are younger or new to a company. I endured a great deal of this, from being sent for 'buckets of steam' or 'sky hooks' to being sent to the local butchers for a 'long wait'. I truly hated this mickey-taking and believe that the perpetrator will never, in the long term, benefit from the best of their victim. And, after all, each time I was sent on a pointless errand, I wasn't earning money **for** my employer, but I was still taking money **from** him.

After two years, again pushed by my brother, I took the huge step off the streets, so to speak, and into Finefare, a regional supermarket chain, as a management trainee. I did well and became a manager before leaving, two years later, to make my biggest geographical move – to the South.

With hindsight, I can see that, at this early stage of my career, I was learning on two fronts. On the one hand I was being taught the very practical skills involved in running a store – organizational skills, planning, stock control, staff scheduling and so on – and, on the other hand, I was beginning to understand how people interacted. Although the latter skill wasn't being formally taught, it was clearly being learnt. I found myself mediating when two groups were not seeing eye-to-eye, consoling people when things went wrong and convincing others when I believed my way was best.

I left Finefare for the same reason that I leave any job – I'd stopped learning. Over the years friends and colleagues have often asked me whether they should leave their jobs and apply for a 'better' one. The advice I offer is always the same. If the decision is driven by a need to grow or learn new skills, it **will be** a good move. If, on the other hand, it is driven merely by a need to earn more then it **may be** a bad one.

After a brief period working for Pontin's (again in their supermarket), a temporary job in a brickyard (not my style, I discovered!) and a 'see the world and have fun' period spent in France, I felt I had finally grown up and achieved independence!

On my return to the UK I attended an interview at Safeway in Bournemouth. I said I'd been a manager at Finefare so, naturally, I wanted to be a manager at Safeway. The assistant manager, Richard Slade, told me that it wasn't that simple. Even to be selected for the management training course you had to be a department manager. I asked him which department had the highest turnover of managers. That was the department I joined the following Monday night – as a shelf filler!

Here was a superb company, way ahead of its time in terms of staff development. I learned a great deal at Safeway and, to this day, it is my longest period of employment with one company. On the technical side, Safeway pushed my thinking into the twentieth century, and much of what I was taught is still relevant today.

My mentor (although such a concept didn't exist in those days) was a certain John Allibone, Store Manager in Bournemouth. I regarded him as my leader and role model and would do, and did, anything he asked of me. I progressed to the position of John's assistant manager and, then, when he and I considered the time was right, I moved on to become a store manager in Poole, Dorset where, with the help of a wonderful group of staff, we turned a long-term loss into a modest profit. After two years as manager (by which time I had worked for Safeway for six years) I moved on yet again. I felt that I had learnt all I could from the environment I was in and, at 25 years old, the thought of being anywhere for too long frightened me.

After a brief attempt at self-employment, which I decided was not for me, I joined BAT, in their stores division, ending up as the Operations Manager for a chain of 'convenience' stores in and around London. Here, for the first time, I was trying to manage remotely – something which I would have found impossible had I not used some of what I now call the Thinking Organization approach.

The company, John Quality, had no plan, very little structure and no formal procedures. This meant that my colleagues and I had to start at the beginning. I remember using what I would now call, loosely, 'brainstorming, clustering, SWOT analysis and force field analysis' techniques to help me, although at that stage I didn't know the technical terms for these processes.

When BAT, realizing that they either had to expand the business or sell it while it was doing well, decided on the latter option, I moved to Sperrings, then the largest convenience store operator in the UK and credited with introducing the concept to this country. Here, I learned a key management skill – never stop asking questions. When Circle K bought Sperrings and its entire staff my job was in licensing and carried the incredible title of Director of Licensed Operations and Oil Development!

During my five years in the convenience store business (three with Sperrings and two with Circle K), I was responsible, along with others, for the establishment, licensing and management of geographical areas, together with the set-up of convenience stores on petrol station forecourts. The first of these, in Richmond, Surrey, is acknowledged as the first forecourt convenience store in the UK. The year was 1986.

Two years later I joined Elf as Marketing Manager – a move which was to create a small stir in the oil industry, because I had apparently come from nowhere. Prior to my appointment 'head of anything' jobs had been filled by 'lifers' progressing through the industry hierarchy.

At that time Elf was seriously considering pulling out of the UK. I was successful in implementing a change in brand image, improving the company's credibility and introducing the first smart-card style promotion in the UK. Elf went on to buy Amoco, and I was being prepared for a move to France. Then, in June 1991, I was headhunted to become the Managing Director of Burmah Petroleum Fuels Ltd (BFPL), a division of Burmah Castrol. BFPL went on to win seven industry awards and, more importantly, outperformed the rest of the sector while it was facing severe competition from the growth of out-of-town hypermarkets selling own-brand petrol.

BFPL features throughout this book because, as Managing Director, I had the opportunity, for the first time, to implement fully the ideas and approaches outlined in this book. Its sale, for what was described as 'full price' (seen as inconceivable four years earlier), gave me the chance to consider achieving in a different area. I decided that it was time I began to spread the word. I wanted to let others know just how easy it is to achieve so much more than is thought possible.

This led me to create Kestrel Consulting Ltd. When putting together a brochure for Kestrel I looked at our USP (unfair selling proposition) and realized that ours was partly the unique product but also the added value derived from my experience as a practitioner. The fact that I have 'done it' and not just thought of it helps me trade at the highest level. I did not want to lose that involvement, so I decided I needed another company to run as a Thinking Organization.

In August 1997 I led a management buy-in into a £50m petroleum retailing company and, in January 1998, made a second acquisition which moved the company to *c.* £150m sales. I have called the company Petrol Express (the name created by my eight-year-old son, Martin).

Because this book is so much a reflection of my personal journey I have tried to summarize myself and what has – unconsciously for most of the time – shaped my own thinking, particularly in relation to managing organizations. This is as simple as:

O   **create an environment where individual cerebral growth and collective winning are the norm; and**

O   **teach thinking.**

I came from an environment where existence was the norm. To 'better yourself' was not something that was frequently discussed but, internally, the idea of improvement was constantly with me. In part, this is because I have an absolute fear of being average, which means that I have to grow to avoid being submerged. Finding a better way of getting things done has allowed me to break out and then progress. That 'better way' has two strands. First, I've worked hard, and still am working hard, on my communication skills. I know now that there are so many different ways of giving, or not giving, a message that it is almost like having to learn a new language each time you talk, write or listen to someone new. Second, I look for untapped potential in people, then get them to recognize and use it. Giving that message, and creating the conditions which will allow people to receive it, is the central theme of this book.

TONY BUZAN

Tony, who is from a very different background to me, was regarded as a rebel at school, coming into frequent conflict with teachers for questioning what was taught and challenging their judgements on who could be regarded as intelligent – or otherwise! Unlike me, however, he went on to pursue an academic career, gaining a double honours degree in Arts and Science before moving on to the early stages of his business career.

A turning point in Tony's life came, when after a few years' working in junior sales, marketing and management 'work/training experience' he was challenged by an elder statesman of the business community with the disconcerting probe, 'Son, if you're so damned smart, why aren't you rich?'

Why indeed? For once, Tony had no rational answer – and thus began a new stage of his thinking/business career and the start of a 25-year journey towards the successful establishment of a growing global enterprise and a position as one of the world's leading management gurus.

Sought after as a management programme speaker, management adviser to companies and corporations worldwide, leading exponent of thinking techniques and the view that anyone can vastly increase their brainpower, Tony is probably most famous for devising Mind Mapping – a thinking technique that mimics the way the brain works and is used increasingly throughout schools and the business world for learning, revision and problem-solving.

Tony's interest in the psychology of learning, thinking and memory has become a lifelong mission. He is the best-selling author of over 50 books on the brain, learning and business. To date his books have been translated into 24 languages and have sold over 3 million copies in over 100 countries. He has also taught creative thinking skills to thousands of students in schools and universities worldwide.

His passion for excellence and belief in the brain's potential is reflected in the Brain Trust charity which he founded. Its objectives are particularly relevant to Thinking Organization and are fundamentally identical to those of this book: 'to promote research into the study of thought processes, the investigation of the mechanics of thinking, manifested in learning, understanding, communication, problem-solving, creativity and decision-making; to disseminate the results of such research and study, to promote generally education and training in cognitive processes and techniques and to develop and exploit new techniques in cognitive processes'.

All in all, Tony is someone I have long admired. He and I share a mission to release the creative potential in all of us. We have travelled very different paths but are basically 'coming from the same place'. The result is the creation of this book, encouraged and mentored by Tony, which shares the knowledge and techniques that will make your business a success.

PART I
CREATING THE ENVIRONMENT

❖

INTRODUCTION TO PART I

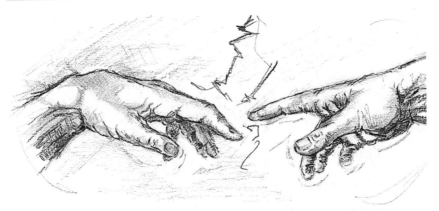

In seeking to create a Thinking Organisation those at the top must first **think!** It is no use trying to achieve higher sales unless consideration has been given to the profit that is required from those sales. That may sound obvious but, to many companies, it is not.

On a more global basis, it is no good motivating a company into a state of frenzy unless you can say where you want the company to be at some stage in the future.

Against this background, Chapter 1, 'Establishing a Framework', presents a more genuinely visual definition of what a 'vision' should be. It also redefines 'mission' and shakes values to death by redefining them as 'Groundrules'. It contains some ideas on whose responsibility it is to create the vision, mission and Groundrules, as well as suggestions about what to do about people who cannot or will not accept the direction you set. Chapter 1 also covers the different ways in which people might fulfil the vision, based on their own personalities, pointing out that varying styles of achievement should not be seen as negative and that, in fact, personal style should be positively encouraged.

Also included are my personal experiences in this area, covering:

○   what drove the need for vision, mission and Groundrules in Burmah Petroleum Fuels Ltd
○   the initial background work
○   what the vision and mission were.

Chapter 2, 'Creating the Culture', explains the Groundrules. These replace outdated values, are cross-departmental, cross-company and cross-cultural and can be remembered by the acronym I O U C H A P:

○   **I**mprovement
○   **O**wnership
○   **U**nderstanding
○   **C**an Do
○   **H**onesty
○   **A**vailability
○   **P**rofessionalism

The chapter covers what the Groundrules are, how they were created and what they will achieve. There are numerous examples – some real, some imaginary. You will relate to the Groundrules because you will instantly see:

○   that they are practically based
○   how, by living them, you as an individual will benefit, as well as the whole company.

You will want to start using them immediately!

This chapter shows you how, without the Groundrules, you cannot create a Thinking Organization. **The Groundrules are the cultural foundation to better thinking**. They are the ultimate facilitator to better internal working relationships. Furthermore, you will understand how all other programmes of a non-technical nature are natural outcomes of living the Groundrules, not the usual forced inputs which most staff ignore or, when the forcing stops, forget.

Chapter 3 offers a simple, but highly effective, marking system for the

Groundrules. When followed on a three-monthly basis, it creates a company where 360° feedback is a term that is not just talked about, but understood and lived. The aim of the marking system is not to produce scientific data that a psychologist could analyse, it is to facilitate an effective conversation between two people who work or live with each other; with actions to follow.

This chapter shows you how turning the company's focus away from the product and even the customers, and clearly focusing on internal and individual relationships means that both product and customers win every time.

Chapter 4 provides further, practical uses for the Groundrules. It introduces the 'Employment Shield', which provides a ready-made 'employee profile'.

Part I, then, is the foundation for creating a Thinking Organization. It concludes with a summary, an all-important action plan, since learning without practice is useless, and a review by Tony Buzan.

1
ESTABLISHING A FRAMEWORK

VISION, MISSION AND GROUNDRULES

Here are three questions which I have asked of many, many people:

1   What is your vision?
2   What is your mission?
3   What are your values?

To date, I have not found anyone who could give me the answers to all three, and it is rare to find more than two members in a group who can even quote their company vision. This is a frightening thought when you consider that the people asked are the senior executives responsible for their creation!

Three problems arise :

1   If senior staff do not know the vision, mission and values how can they expect anyone else to? If, of course, they don't expect anyone else to know them, why have them in the first place?
2   If senior staff do not know the vision, mission or values, how are decisions made in that company? Against what framework? The result is a continuous struggle to survive – that is, to stand still. These organizations may never move forward.
2   The same can be said of any individual. Without a vision for personal growth you aren't going anywhere.

The reason why most people can't quote vision and mission statements is basically because these statements are not memorable and they are too long. I have found that for a vision and mission to be memorable they must be achievable, inspiring, short and visual. I also feel that the mission statement should be translated as a strategy, not as a statement of 'what we do.'

Using pictures to visualize vision, mission and values (Groundrules) is a great help. The following are my definitions and pictures for these key elements.

○   **Vision**. A vision is a future goal. It is what you are striving towards.

The picture I use for this is a **flag** that we are all moving towards.

○   **Mission**. There is little point in using a mission statement to describe the business. Instead, it should represent 'how to achieve the vision'. In other words, having chosen where to go, the next step has to be to decide how to get there.

The company mission is, in effect, the company strategy. Departmental mission statements describe how that department's strategy will contribute towards the achievement of the overall strategy (mission).

I visualise a mission as a **vehicle** taking us from where we are to where we are going.

○   **Groundrules**. These are the replacement for values. They represent the way you want your organization to behave as it drives the vehicle (mission) in order to arrive at the flag (vision).

I see the Groundrules as a **driver's manual**. It is no good having people who know where to go, giving them a vehicle to get there and then not teaching them how to drive it!

RESPONSIBILITY

Much has been written on whose responsibility it is to do what in the area of vision, mission and values. I can only offer my own view, as someone who's done it rather than written about it (to date)!

The **vision** must be driven by the person at the top of the organization, since unless it is driven from the top it is likely to falter in tougher climates. It follows that the leader must create the vision. It will be created as a result of conversations with other people and with the company's own senior personnel, as well as other information, but it must be the Principal's vision. It is difficult to imagine any Principal who could cope with implementing someone else's vision. **A collectively defined vision is no vision at all. It is consensus, which is average and gets you nowhere**.

The **mission**, on the other hand, I believe should be created by the Board. Having decided where you are going, each member of your most senior team should write a strategy which summarizes how their function/department is going to help you reach the flag. From those 'substrategies' the senior team, collectively with the Principal, can devise a simple mission statement which encompasses all those departmental strategies or missions. This overall mission must be accepted on both an intellectual and emotional level by all your management.

Responsibilities
O   **Vision**: *the Principal (that is, the CEO, President, Managing Director)*
O   **Mission**: *the Board (that is, the senior team, titled directors, vice-presidents and so on)*

The **Groundrules** (values) already exist and will fit any organization, large or small, no matter what its business vision and mission. They are the result of over 10 years' work and are the written output of many discussions at all levels. They are therefore a collectively driven set of values. This works because no one person's view of how all should act is going to be acceptable to all.

The Groundrules already exist and are universal. It is important that the Board lives them.

What should you do if there are some people who aren't achieving your vision, mission or Groundrules? There are two answers here.

1   If you are running towards the vision and there are people running with you who fall over, pick them up and help them.

2   If, however, you come across someone who is running away from the vision, mission or values (Groundrules) move them on.

Only if everyone is pulling together, all going the same way, can you expect to get anywhere near your vision. Anybody in your company doing anything to stop that movement towards your flag must be dealt with.

The starting point has to be encouragement to help them understand that your destination is the right one, but this process can't last for ever. The company's external reality is the big world of competition and pressure for results. In-fighting is harmful if not tackled and, unlike external competition, it is within your control. You owe it to those who share your vision to deal with those who don't.

ROUTES

Having said that everyone must actively aim for the same flag, it must be recognized that the route chosen by each individual has to allow for individual, personal, style. There are many different ways of getting from A to Z. As long we share the same destination, how we get there is largely irrelevant.

EXAMPLE
Some people, like myself, see the flag and just run straight towards it. Good points about this style are:

O   It's quick.
O   It's dynamic.
O   It surprises the competition.

Its bad points are:

O   It might mean running straight into a 'minefield'.
O   It might mean falling down holes.

O   It might mean turning around and finding I haven't brought anyone with me.

Others might zigzag, pausing for a while to stop and think, working out other strategies to go forward again. This style, again, has advantages:

O   It's more likely to bring other people along with it.
O   It's more likely to avoid 'minefields' on the way.

It also has disadvantages:

O   It's slower.
O   It's frustrating.
O   It allows the competition more time to read the situation.

Other routes to the flag may include going in a straight line, but stopping to evaluate each new piece of information or just going forward, but very slowly!

As long as everyone is going for the flag, you can, and must, allow for individuality.

BURMAH PETROLEUM FUELS LTD
In order to create a vision for Burmah Petroleum Fuels Ltd (BPFL), I wanted to be clear about my starting point. Before thinking about 'where I wanted to be', I wanted as much information as possible about 'where I was'. I therefore commissioned research into the current and future marketplace, and what was driving this (technology, cost, geography, competition, politics and so on). This exercise provided some information which was ultimately key in deciding the vision. For example, the company did not know that it was, at that time, no. 3 in a specific (dealer) marketplace. In fact, in certain geographical areas, it was no. 1 or 2. The company's focus and its money had, historically, been concentrated in another (company-owned) area of the marketplace where it was competing with oil industry giants, such as Shell and Esso. This led me to the conclusion that I was more likely to be successful if I created a new focus where I was generally not fighting with the giants.

At the end of the process I defined my vision for BPFL as:

'To be the number one supplier to the independent dealer market in the United Kingdom.'

I then worked, with my directors, on formulating the mission. What did we need to do to achieve our vision? Our conclusion was summarized as:

'To deliver the vision through the implementation of the "Dealer's Dealer" strategy.'

The 'Dealer's Dealer' was a tag-line which said that we were focusing on the dealer, but also that we would act with understanding of the dealer. This would get us to the no. 1 position. Dealers would come to us because we considered their point of view. The substance of the strategy was a whole range of services (some new to the industry) which would be offered to the dealers.

The Groundrules (values), as I have said, were the output of many discussions and 'thinking' sessions. In BPFL I also had to consider the Groundrules within the overall Burmah Castrol corporation. Burmah Castrol had its own set of values which were more than covered by the Groundrules. It accepted that its values were an 'umbrella' under which divisions would work. My plan was ultimately to convince Burmah Castrol that one set of Groundrules could serve the Group, worldwide.

CONCLUSION

This first chapter has looked at the need for an organization to create and focus on a very clear vision and mission. Many employees, if asked, would be unable to state their company's vision or mission, but most could give a very clear description of the operational controls under which they work. This reflects the common situation in which a company has an unclear vision but tight operational controls.

My own way is the reverse of this: a very clear vision and mission with a loose framework of 'self-control'. By this I mean that employees, given clear direction through a strong vision, will create their own controls over the processes needed to achieve that vision. Ironically, this type of control is usually tighter and more strictly enforced than the normal 'imposed' control.

A workforce empowered to create its own systems and processes of control will not waste time or energy trying to 'work round' the system. They also adjust and update those controls without being prompted – the vision stays the same; the means of achieving it will vary over time.

I have called this 'loose framework' of controls the Groundrules which are explained in the following chapter. They are, essentially, values for the twenty-first century, which, if implemented fully, will provide you with a means of releasing and directing the energy and intellectual capital of everyone in your Thinking Organization.

2
CREATING THE CULTURE

❖

The catalyst for the Thinking Organization was not so much the thinking techniques that were taught (more of which later), but that they were taught in conjunction with the development and implementation of the company's values. Originally these values were called 'Business Groundrules'. However, because the Groundrules that exist today are universal, transferable between work and home, intercompany, interdepartment and intercultural, they became known simply as the 'Groundrules'.

The Groundrules or values, as stated earlier, were the driver's manual to take the vehicle (mission) on its destination towards the flag (vision). They did not just leap from pen to paper; they started off in a very basic format and developed over time, based on experience in implementing them. They also have their own marking system, which throws out traditional, annual appraisals (designed, it seems to me, as a form of wage control – a typical appraisal being 'Rikki, I've been meaning to tell you that you're doing a lousy job and your pay rise is 1 per cent') and replaces them with quarterly, one-to-one, two-way reviews of the working relationship, not the tasks.

The Groundrules help create an environment where the Thinking Organization can flourish.

These are the roots, the foundation, the base, the 'everything-there-is' to the creation of a culture in which a Thinking Organization emerges and flourishes. Thinking techniques, as you will discover later, are important but lose their maximum impact if taught in isolation and in the wrong environment. If you take thinking techniques and place them in the environment created by the Groundrules using those techniques becomes 'the norm'. The result is an unbeatable combination.

The Groundrules bypass company politics. They replace company values that encompass many old value terms – such as 'loyalty' and 'respect' – which are still relevant but are just misunderstood. Because the Groundrules are understandable, they are more easily lived by everyone in an organization.

THE GROUNDRULES

We will be known in all of our individual relationships, both personal and professional, for:

IMPROVEMENT

All individuals are seen to be **continuously** seeking to **improve relationships, processes, themselves** and the **company's performance**.

OWNERSHIP

We approach the way in which we make and take decisions as if we **owned the company**, its **direction, successes** and **problems** and as if we were **spending our own money**.

UNDERSTANDING

We work hard to understand by **listening** to the position of each party in any of our relationships. We **value differences** and **accept** that they, like us, will have objectives and motivations.

'CAN DO' APPROACH

We are **positive** in looking for ways in which we can **help each other** do what we believe is right for the company. We can demonstrate that we **consider alternatives**.

HONESTY

We **do what we say we will**, with defined but **not hidden agendas** and regard being **open and honest about ourselves** and **others** as crucial.

AVAILABILITY

You can **get to us**, we will **return your call**, we **respond to your messages**, you **know where we are**.

PROFESSIONALISM

We show **attention to detail**, are **well prepared, knowledgeable** in our subject, and **focused** in terms of our objectives and priorities.

EXPLANATION AND EXAMPLES OF THE GROUNDRULES

Each Groundrule has a summarizing **keyword** and a number of **subwords** which are shown in bold type. Understanding these subwords is the basis of interpreting the Groundrules correctly, so a separate explanation and/or example of every subword is given below.

KEYWORD: **IMPROVEMENT**

All individuals are seen to be **continuously** seeking to **improve relationships**, **processes**, **themselves** and the **company's performance**.

Subword: 'continuously'

Explanation/example   Not improvement when it suits, improvement every third Sunday or every full moon – **continuous** improvement.

Sub-word: 'relationships'

Explanation/example   If you were reprimanded in front of other people then the **relationship** between you and the person who reprimanded you is going to suffer. If, as your line manager, I have problems because my peers are complaining about something you did, then our **relationship** will suffer.

Subword: 'processes'

Explanation/example   It is not acceptable to use the phrase 'We've always done it that way'. If you are not continually seeking to improve **processes**; if you can't demonstrate that the **process** you use today is the best on the market, then you are not living this part of the Groundrule.

Sub-word: 'themselves'

Explanation/example

*All individuals must take responsibility to develop **themselves**. It is not the company's responsibility – the company doesn't own your intellect or your direction. **The company's responsibility is to facilitate the growth of your intellect**.*

Subwords: 'company's performance'

Explanation/example   We don't work for a laugh – the fact that we have a laugh is a pleasant byproduct. We actually work for money. The wealth of our company will determine its future. We must work towards improving the **company's performance** in every area we can think of, be that financial or non-financial. An example of a way in which non-financial performance can be affected is if I upset you so much that your performance and that of those below you is affected.

KEYWORD: **OWNERSHIP**

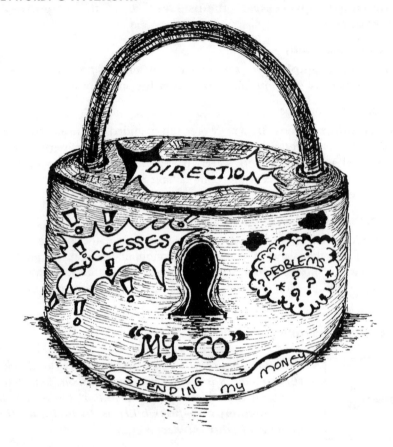

We approach the way in which we make and take decisions as if we **owned the company**, its **direction**, **successes** and **problems** and as if we were **spending our own money**.

Subwords: 'owned the company'

Explanation/example   It is fair to say that if everybody **owned the company** in which they made the decisions, they wouldn't make half of the foolish decisions that they do.

Subword: 'direction'

Explanation/example   This word allows you to be quite clear with others that unless they can accept where you are going, there is no position for them in your company. I cannot emphasize enough that there is no place for people pulling in the other **direction**. Whether they are proven to be right in hindsight is irrelevant. During the process, if they do not convince you to change **direction**, or do not support you, then they must be dealt with.

Subword: 'successes'

Explanation/example   Be proud of **successes**. It's an important part of feeling good about yourself and reinforcing willingness to take decisions. Again, ways of celebrating **successes** are individual. Some will want to stand up and say 'I did that', 'I made that decision', 'I created that opportunity', or 'I took advantage of that opportunity', while others will just want to tell a few people. What is important is not to put down someone for being pleased with what they have achieved, but to see it as part of getting everyone to the flag and recognizing individuality.

Subword: 'problems'

Explanation/example   How many times have you seen people pass the buck? Too often, I'm sure. A better way is to say 'oops! Got that wrong, and here's a way out of what I've got us into'. Taking ownership of **problems** genuinely allows the creation of further opportunities. The ownership of **problems** is helped by an environment in which mistakes are allowed to be made without you being beaten up for them. But to earn that right you must first demonstrate that ownership.

Subwords: 'spending our own money'

Explanation/example   If I were to have a budget for staying in hotels, then whether I stay in an economy or de-luxe hotel would be a matter of individual preference and judgement. As long as we behave as if we were **spending our own money**, this Groundrule allows for individual preference. If, for example, a Sales Director sends out a directive insisting that everyone stays 'economy', the point has been missed. If, on the other hand, the directive states that everyone should stay within budget, that's different. Interpreting how that budget should be spent by setting out a 'code of accommodation', is wrong because it removes responsibility, and therefore ownership, for the decisions an individual makes. Out of two people, one may enjoy caravanning holidays and is quite prepared to sleep in a more basic environment. The other may enjoy de-luxe holidays and save all year to afford one. This Groundrule allows each of those individuals, with their differing tastes, to trade within the same area. If the 'de-luxe' person has no money left by June they have to pay for themselves – it's their choice.

This approach makes people responsible for all the decisions they make. If you don't trust others to be as wise as yourself, then don't give them a budget in the first place. This clearly, as I am sure you will see, facilitates true empowerment – the authority and willingness to take decisions and ownership of the responsibility that goes with it.

KEYWORD: **UNDERSTANDING**

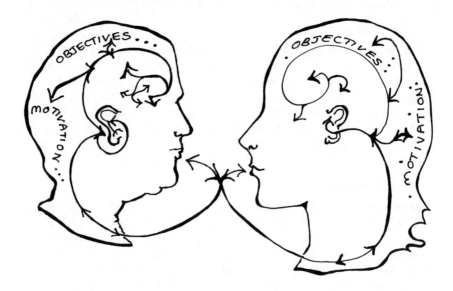

We work hard to understand by **listening** to the position of each party in any of our relationships. We **value differences** and **accept** that they, like us, will have objectives and motivations.

Subword: 'listening'

Explanation/example   How many times have you come across someone hearing, but not **listening**? A mind already made up, but 'going through the motions'? Someone only waiting for the other person to finish in order to speak? In his book, *Principle Centred Leadership*, Stephen Covey says that 'we should seek first to understand and second to be understood.' To achieve this, we must demonstrate that we listen.

Subwords: 'value differences'

Explanation/example   There must be different types of people in an effective team. We all have differences; we all have different approaches. You must **value differences** as well as recognise that they exist. Don't just accept them passively, regard them as something wholly positive. If your competitors have average managers who do things as they have always been done and you have managers who will consider alternatives, you are the one with the absolute advantage. Value and use that advantage. Go out and search for people who are different and then recruit them!

Subword: 'accept'

Explanation/example   Although not always convenient, it is a fact that we all differ in our objectives and motivations – we have different reasons for doing things. This has to be understood and **accepted** because it will help you identify what motivates each person. Again, positively **accept** and embrace this fact and you will have a better, more effective, team.

KEYWORD: 'CAN DO' APPROACH

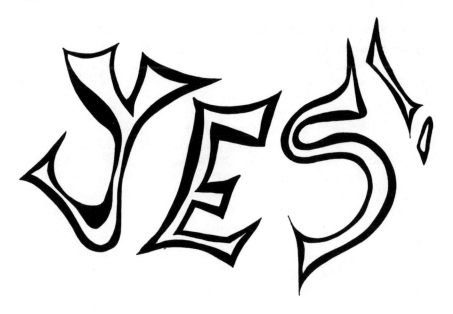

We are **positive** in looking for ways in which we can **help each other** do what we believe is right for the company. We can demonstrate that we **consider alternatives**.

Subword: 'positive'

Explanation/example   In every conversation the starting point must be a **positive** 'yes'. It may not be the immediate response because we may not know how to achieve what we are being asked to achieve but the initial reaction should be 'Yes, we will do it', 'Yes, it can be done', 'Yes I can achieve that'. This approach is especially effective at the middle and lower levels of an organization.

Subwords: 'help each other'

Explanation/example   If you imagine a salesperson saying to a finance person, 'Here's what I want to do' and the finance person says, 'Right, I'll help you', what would happen next? You'd realize it was a dream and instantly wake up!

However, it doesn't need to be like that. If you create the right environment, you will see individuals **help each other** to achieve the vision. A group of staff and managers – cross-functional, cross-hierarchical – all working together with a 'can do' approach is a wonderful sight. The achievements can be phenomenal.

Subwords: 'consider alternatives'

Explanation/example   Although the starting point is always 'Yes, we can do that' and, in many cases an immediate 'Yes, it can be done', there are also occasions when the response has to be 'Well, OK, I know what you're trying to achieve but I need to think about it, and I'll come back to you'.

When you do come back, you can demonstrate that you've tried to make the proposition work by **considering alternatives**. Of course, you may have found a way of achieving what is required exactly as has been suggested; alternatively, you might say 'Well, I can't do it exactly the way you asked, but here's another way of achieving it'. A third possibility is that you have to say 'It's actually possible, but it's illegal' or 'It's possible, but we'll go broke if we do it – here's why.'

However, there will be two important differences in reaction to these alternative responses in an organization which lives the Groundrules. First, you will be believed because it is obvious that you positively tried to make it happen. Second, your working relationship will not be damaged by any decision not to proceed. But, in such an environment, it's still odds-on that you will think of an option!

KEYWORD: HONESTY

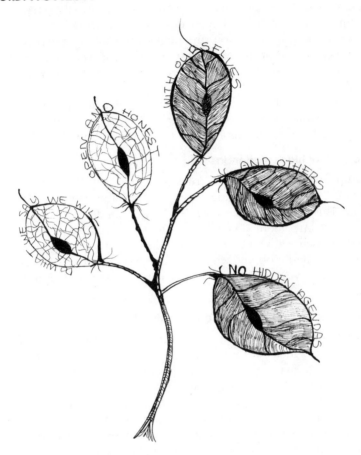

We **do what we say we will**, with defined but **not hidden agendas** and regard being **open and honest about ourselves** and **others** as crucial.

Subwords: 'do what we say we will'

Explanation/example   Sniping and backbiting is not acceptable. It is not acceptable to say one thing in a meeting and then go say something else outside. The Uriah Heep approach does not work.

Let's assume that you've attended a meeting and a course of action has been decided with which you violently disagree. You return to your team and say, as a good Director, 'Here's where we're going as a company ...' and your team protests, 'But, boss, that's crazy. That's just not right, it won't work.' Your traditional response may be 'I know. I told them all, they didn't listen, so we've got to do what they want'.

However, this attitude does nothing to encourage people to pull in the same direction. Now, of course, it would be equally dishonest to say 'I think this is a great idea,' if you don't think it is. What you can say, however, is 'I hear what you are saying, and all of the points you're making were raised at the meeting. On balance it has been decided that this is the way we're going, so let's get on with it and **do what we say we will.**'

This approach allows you to demonstrate that the points have been raised, but a direction has been chosen. That must be the direction in which you all travel, not passively, but with vigour and enthusiasm.

Subwords: 'not hidden agendas'

Explanation/example It is a cruel fact of life that Principals and senior Operating Executives sometimes have to hold information that they can't pass on. This is perfectly acceptable. This Groundrule allows us to say, when asked 'Are there going to be any more redundancies?', 'I'm not allowed to discuss it with you'. To say 'I don't know', when you do, would be dishonest and nobody would believe you anyway. Saying 'I can't discuss it with you' is honest. It is having a defined but **not hidden agenda**.

Subwords: 'open and honest about ourselves'

Explanation/example We must be **open and honest about ourselves**; we must acknowledge our shortcomings, realize that our improvement hasn't been all that it should be, recognize that we're not taking ownership, or just not working hard at understanding – whatever is the issue. We must be honest with ourselves; otherwise, we will never develop and progress. Incidentally, who else are you cheating but yourself? Furthermore, if we are **honest about ourselves**, others will be more prepared to listen to us when we are being honest with them.

Subword: 'others'

Explanation/example We should follow the Groundrules in our dealings with everyone, not just our work colleagues. We must be honest with all **others** – our customers, suppliers, peers, subordinates, superiors, family and friends. An example of dishonesty is the practice followed by some companies of stringing along suppliers or perhaps people seeking sponsorship, in the knowledge they have no intention whatsoever of taking that service or sponsoring that individual.

Sometimes people are uncomfortable in being honest about **others** because they may need to give an unwelcome judgement or assessment and see it as 'giving bad news' which will upset the person on the receiving end. Look at this in another, more positive, way. You are honest with someone because you care enough about them to want them to have the information so that they can improve. Clearly, how the message is conveyed is important. Even 'bad' news can be handled with compassion. The alternative is not to be honest; to leave false perceptions in place and ultimately decrease that person's chances of winning.

KEYWORD: **AVAILABILITY**

You can **get to us**, we will **return your call**, we **respond to your messages**, you **know where we are**.

Subwords: 'get to us'

Explanation/example   How many people maintain that they operate an 'open door' policy? I know of one Director who always left his office door open, but kept the light switched off. What sort of message did that send to the outside world? How many people say 'You can **get to us**', but they are so miserable and unwelcoming that you wouldn't want to get to them in the first place? To live this Groundrule not only should you give others physical access, you also have to create an atmosphere around you that says 'Yes, I want you to talk to me'.

Subwords: 'return your call'

Explanation/example   When messages are taken we should guarantee that we will **return your call**. We may not do this personally, but we should contact the person for whom we took the message and follow up to make sure that a return call has been made. There is no point in politely taking a message for someone else, and either failing to pass it on or make sure that some action has taken place. Even if you do not want to make that return call, you must. Not to do so is sending the wrong message – not just externally but internally as well – and it won't be long before someone does the same to you.

Subwords: 'respond to your messages'

Explanation/example   If you've written to me I will write back – I will **respond to your message**. As Chairman of Swindon Town Football Club I make a point of responding in detail to every single letter within 10 days. As you can imagine, with a football club, few of these are letters of support!

Subwords: 'know where we are'

Explanation/example   How many of us fail to inform our secretaries, peers, managers or family of our whereabouts? Letting people **know where we are** makes the company look professional and certainly stops telephone lines being clogged up while the operator calls department after department looking for you! There is no excuse, with today's modern communication methods, for not being available. Being available is seen as highly professional by customers – yet few practise it.

KEYWORD: PROFESSIONALISM

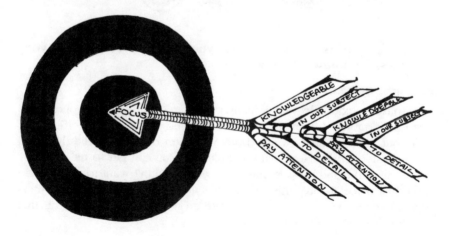

We show **attention to detail**, are **well prepared, knowledgeable** in our subject and **focused** in terms of our objectives and priorities.

Subwords: 'attention to detail'

Explanation/example So much money, time and effort is wasted because somebody has not paid **attention to detail**, which results in more work to put things right.

Subwords: 'well prepared'

Explanation/example Make sure that, when you attend meetings, you've done your homework. There is nothing more disrespectful than to turn up at a meeting not having read the papers sent out in advance. Being **well prepared** gives others confidence that what you are saying is based on well thought-through plans.

Subword: 'knowledgeable'

Explanation/example Be **knowledgeable** about the subject under discussion – do not bullshit, do not pretend that you know something you don't but, equally, do not feel that you *must* know something. It's quite acceptable to say at a meeting 'I don't know a lot about this subject, but this is how I feel …'. You gain much more respect with that approach than by saying something which is obviously based on lack of knowledge.

Subword: 'focused'

Explanation/example Narrow the target down, get to the point and move on. Use a rifle, not shotgun, approach to doing business. **Focus** on what the objective is, **focus** on what the priority is, **focus** on what the project is and deal with that. The big picture is important but to execute it you must **focus** on the target.

The key to the Groundrules is that they are understandable common sense and are transferable between work and home. Those living them are not being asked to act differently at work and at home. They are, in a sense, natural laws – a way we should all really be living if we are following a sensible lifestyle.

3

APPRAISING PERFORMANCE

THE GROUNDRULES REVIEW: BACKGROUND

Having explained the Groundrules in some detail, it would be easy to stop there. However, any system or approach must be audited. It is this which facilitates long-term success and it is this which prevents the Groundrules from being just another 'fad'.

The concept of regular appraisals is a good one, particularly if they are two-way. Unfortunately, the process has been abused and, appraisals nowadays, are, frankly, viewed by many employees as a way of keeping their salaries down.

Consider the usual appraisal scenario. Every year you sit down with your manager who tells you how average or poor your performance has been. Sometimes you're told 'You've done OK' and this is followed by a 1 per cent pay increase. It's at the appraisal interview that you often learn, for the first time, that what you've been doing wasn't what was wanted or up to standard. So, it isn't surprising that when you talk to people about appraisals, let alone '360°' appraisals, they cringe.

How do you tell your manager what you really think when this is the first time you've sat down together since the last appraisal – usually a year ago? By the same token, how can you be expected to have a 'free and frank discussion' about your future development? An appraisal usually makes you feel that you'll be lucky to arrive home with a job, let alone a future!

Appraisals in isolation are unlikely to work. What is needed is a framework to create a daily environment which facilitates two-way discussion. The Groundrules provide this framework. By focusing on the relationship between you and your manager or between you and your staff member they provide the means for a structured discussion of that relationship. This structured discussion is called the Groundrules Review. This type of review differs from an appraisal in the following ways:

○   It focuses on the relationship, not the tasks or objective. This does not mean that you do not tackle tasks or objectives as part of the normal management process. However, unless you build the right relationship you will never get the best out of the person you are asking to perform those tasks. Sort out the relationship and the rest is easy.

○   It is individual in two ways.

   –   First, the only relationship that you review is that between yourself and the other person. This is the only relationship on which you are qualified to comment. Your views on your subordinate's relationship with someone else can only be based on an incomplete picture.

   –   Second, it is individual in the sense that it is sufficiently dynamic to reflect all the types of change that take place in a relationship, caused by circumstances, changes in job and so on. The process allows the nature of each relationship to be determined by the two people concerned but, at the same time, retains overall control of the culture by saying that the relationship must be conducted within the Groundrules.

THE GROUNDRULES REVIEW PROCESS

Every **three months**, not annually, you and your manager or staff member sit down with the Groundrules and mark each other against them. The system is simple. Some time before the meeting each of you completes one of the forms shown in the Appendix to this chapter (pp. 40–42). You will see that this has a section for general conversation and a section for Groundrules discussion, including examples and action plans. You would attend the meeting having completed Section One on page 40 (General Discussion) and Section Two on page 42 (your views on how the other person is living the Groundrules). At the meeting you give the other person your views and they give you theirs, which you copy on to your sheet as you go. The point of the exercise is to facilitate a discussion about your individual relationship and agree how to improve it. The Groundrules provide the framework for that discussion.

EXAMPLES OF MARKING AGAINST THE GROUNDRULES

Here are two worked examples to show the main principles of marking against the Groundrules. A complete copy of the review forms is given in the Appendix to this chapter.

Example 1: Improvement

Taking the Groundrule key word, **improvement**, pick out the subwords which are highlighted (**continuously** seeking to improve **relationships**, **processes**, **themselves** and the **company's performance**). Against each of these highlighted words put a tick or a cross. To put a cross you must have an example of the other person not living that part of the Groundrule during the period under review.

Continuously   Assume a tick for **continuously** (seeking). Seeking, whilst not highlighted, is an important word because of what it adds to the meaning. It recognizes that it is not always possible to achieve improvement. What we are looking for here is people who are trying – not always succeeding, but **continuously** seeking.

Relationships   There may be an occasion on which the other person let you down. Maybe they caused you a problem in another department; maybe they insulted you in front of others. If there is such an example put a cross against the word **relationships** and write something like 'insults' under the Examples section on the form, to remind you for the discussion.

Processes   You may have examples of how the other person's department is not seeking to improve its processes and give an illustration of how this is not helping us move forward. There may be a reporting process for keeping each other informed which they have not followed.

Themselves   You may tick this subword because you know that the other person is working on their own development.

The company's performance   You may tick this phrase because, on the whole, you would say, 'Yes, they're facing the right way, and they're working hard on achieving the results and targets we have set ourselves.'

Out of the five highlighted words and phrases you now have three ticks and two crosses. With an allocation of 10 points representing 100 per cent, three ticks would be 6 out of 10. More importantly, it allows you to give the other person examples of why you have marked them down in some areas. The point of filling this in, in advance, is that the pre-work – such as thinking of your examples – facilitates the openness that is needed to use the system. You can think about what you want to say and how to say it.

The whole rationale behind the form is the conversation. Thus the exact nature of 'points' is irrelevant except to provide the key areas for you to consider in that particular relationship. The document is used by you alone.

Example 2: Ownership

Owned the company   You tick this because the other person generally lives as if they do own this company.

Direction   You give another tick because you believe that the other person is aiming for the flag and is demonstrating their belief in the direction chosen.

Successes   The other person may receive a cross here because when you had a success (a new customer) their attitude was 'That's what you're paid for'. This response will not encourage you to work hard for success.

Problems   There may be a few times you've heard the other person say 'It was down to my finance manager' or 'It was the marketing guy'. You may not however, be sure, so just because you have a feeling that they are not accepting any of the problems as theirs, you put a straight line against **problems**. This highlights that you want to have a discussion about this with the other person to find out whether or not they're passing the buck. From a marking point of view this dash represents a half-point, but, after the conversation, you might tick it because you have been convinced they are accepting the problems as their own.

Spending our own money   If you tick these subwords it is because you perceive the other person accounts for money as if it were their own.

Out of the five highlighted words and phrases you have allocated three ticks, one cross and one line. However, you do not have to give the same value to each of the five subsections to the Ownership Groundrule. You can weight what you consider to be important. This could be particularly applicable, when marking the Groundrule, for example, **Availability**. Some people regard **'You can get to us'** as very important because they need a great deal of your time. Others don't, so it is not seen as so important. Although they may have an example of when you weren't available for them they may just be pointing it out – knocking off just one point – because it has less impact on them than on others.

Having arrived at a score for each of the Groundrules you then transpose those scores on to the 'Shape of Relationship' graph (see Figure 3.1) so that when you attend the meeting you have a pre-thought out conversation, with examples.

Once you have both discussed, for example, **'Improvement'** you will both have two lines on the 'Shape of Relationship' graph. All this does, at

Shape of Relationship

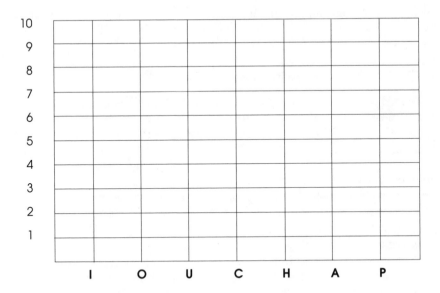

Plot: A) The score for the person you are reviewing (before you meet).

Plot: B) The score they give you. (Use different colours for each)

Figure 3.1   The shape of the relationship graph

the end of the discussion, is show where there are gaps and where you will both agree to consider your relationship.

This is the key to the success of the Groundrules – the process is personal and it's relational.

However, it isn't always necessary to take action to close any large gaps revealed on the chart. For example, you may have scored the other person high on **Availability** while they've scored you low. But they may also say 'Look, although I've made this comment, it's no big deal to me. I don't need you to work on it for the next three months'. Where you both agree that one of you needs to take some action, this is written in the relevant box. As a result you both leave the meeting feeling totally honest, relieved, relaxed and that **there is an outcome**.

For the next meeting in three months' time, a new form is completed. You can start the Groundrules session by talking about the action points from the previous meeting – if you want to. Again, this is a matter of individual choice, not a 'must do,' and should generally take only a few minutes.

THE PERFECT '10'

You could be forgiven for thinking that the aim of the Groundrules Review is, over time, to achieve consistent scores of '10' across the board – that perhaps this is some kind of 'target'. However …

A reality check

I was once in a meeting in which a group of people were trying to convince me that the world of our business was all sunshine and sweetness. A perfect 10. Suddenly I began to fake a minor fit, causing my colleagues, who were unaware that it was fake, some concern. After 30 seconds or so, I picked myself up and plonked my backside on to a chair. Wiping the pretend perspiration from my brow, I said, 'Sorry about that, but from time to time I have bouts of realism. What you just saw was a "reality fit".'

I went on to explain that whilst I agree with taking a positive view of the world, the fact is that, occasionally, obstacles make life less than perfect. I suggested that the point in the business cycle at which we then found ourselves could turn against us, so some pre-thought about what we would do would not go amiss. I then proposed that they Mind Mapped the issues surrounding a potential downturn. In accordance with the nature of cycles the market did eventually downturn and our company was positioned to minimize damage.

Relating this story to the 'perfect 10', I would say that, as humans, we are the perfect creation and may well be able to progress to individual perfection. However, perfection is a matter of individual judgement, rather like success, and, as such, is individually measured. This means that when we interact with others we are putting together a highly subjective view of the same issue: what 'A' thinks is acceptable behaviour might be unacceptable to 'B'.

Furthermore, we are 'human' – not 'only human' but 'human' – and I have yet to meet anyone who gets everything right all the time. Even though I am quite obviously an exceptional person in many ways I am not, alas, perfect in the eyes of others!

Equally, we react to others based on how they react to us. Although we might like to think that if someone verbally attacked us we would react in a pleasant manner, it is just not reality. Our reactions are based not only on how we think but also on how we feel – and we don't always feel the same.

The goal of the Groundrules Review is to facilitate a conversation between two individuals using a common language – that of the Groundrules. It addresses concerns and barriers that exist in that relationship and which, if left undiscussed, would stop the creation of the desired culture.

The system must not become a 'points scoring' exercise or a 'pointless' exercise in proving that you are perfect. It represents real human beings in real situations and, as a result, helps them make those relationships effective. It avoids falling into the trap of 'fad' management in which the system rules rather than being a tool.

Anyone having a consistantly straight line score on the 'Shape of Relationship' graph, either high or low, has not been fairly assessed by the other person. The individual in this situation is given to believe that they are either generally OK or generally poor. In reality no-one is that good or that bad all the time. Over time, reviews between the same two people will have different shapes – just as our relationships with anyone have their 'ups and downs'. In effect, the Groundrules Review system is rather like one of those toys where you push one component down and another pops up because they are all connected.

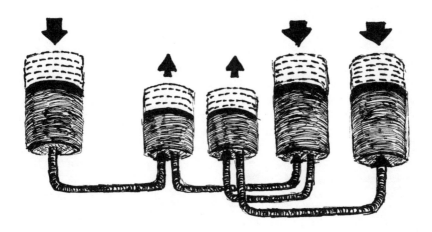

Dynamics example

Taking the point made under 'The perfect 10' a bit further, the Groundrules are dynamic in how they impact on each other.

For example, if I had done something without communicating it to you when I should, then you could put a cross against me under keyword **Improvement**, subwords **continuously**, **relationships** and **processes**. Equally, I could be crossed under keyword **Understanding**, subword **listening**, as well as keyword **Honesty**, subwords **do what we say we will** and, possibly, **not hidden agendas**.

APPENDIX: THE GROUNDRULES REVIEW

Notes on completing review sheet

- Score the person you are reviewing on the basis of **your relationship with them**.

- Each Groundrule has highlighted components. Mark each highlighted comment with a tick (if you are satisfied this is happening), with a cross (if you have an example of this not happening) or a dash (if, whilst you might not have an example, you have a concern and wish to discuss).

- Calculate ticks as a percentage of the total possible (one tick possible for each highlighted statement) e.g. 3 ticks out of 6 equals 5 out of 10. (A dash is 1/2.) 'Weighting' based on personal priorities can be used to make the system even more individual.

- Plot the score on the 'Shape of Relationship' grid. Then check to see that the points reflect how you feel about your relationship under each Groundrule. If the points are not high or low enough – change them – but make a note under the 'Examples' section to explain why you have weighted it.

- Make sure you have noted your examples.

- Following your discussion agree action points.

Groundrules Review

Name   Date
(of person being reviewed)

Initial, general discussion – approx. timing 30 minutes

Free section to raise any issue – work or personal

A) Your issues . . . .
. . . .
. . . .

B) Other person's issues
. . . .
. . . .
. . . .

Shape of Relationship

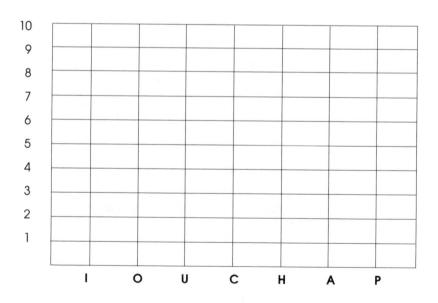

Plot: A) The score for the person you are reviewing (before you meet).
Plot: B) The score they give you. (Use different colours for each)

GROUNDRULES

We will be known in all of our relationships, both personal and professional, for:

IMPROVEMENT

All individuals and groups of individuals are seen to be **continuously** seeking to **improve relationships, processes, themselves** and the **company's performance**.

OWNERSHIP

We approach the way in which we make and take decisions as if we **owned the company**, its **direction, successes** and **problems** and as if we were **spending our own money**.

UNDERSTANDING

We work hard to understand by **listening** to the position of each party in any of our relationships. We **value differences** and **accept** that they, like us, will have objectives and motivations.

'CAN DO' APPROACH

We are **positive** in looking for ways in which we **can help each other** do what we believe is right for the company. We can demonstrate that we **consider alternatives**.

HONESTY

We **do what we say we will**, with defined but **not hidden agendas** and regard being **open and honest about ourselves** and **others** as crucial.

AVAILABILITY

You can **get to us**, we will **return your call**, we **respond to your messages**, you **know where we are**.

PROFESSIONALISM

We show **attention to detail**, are **well prepared, knowledgeable** in our subject, and **focused** in terms of our objectives and priorities.

I	Example(s)
	Action(s) Self Other person
O	Example(s)
	Action(s) Self Other person
U	Example(s)
	Action(s) Self Other person
C	Example(s)
	Action(s) Self Other person
H	Example(s)
	Action(s) Self Other person
A	Example(s)
	Action(s) Self Other person
P	Example(s)
	Action(s) Self Other person

4

PUTTING THE GROUNDRULES TO WORK

THE EMPLOYMENT SHIELD

I once gave a presentation on recruitment to a group of petrol station owners. I had two chairs on a stage and moved from chair to chair as I interviewed a mock employee. The conversation went something like this:

Employer. 'Hello. Do you have two arms that work?'

Employee. 'Yes.'
Employer. 'Do you have two legs which work?'
Employee. 'Yes?'
Employer. 'Well, you're late – you should have been here at nine!'

Clearly this is an exaggeration of the way most interviews are conducted, but I don't think it's much of one.

Many problems in a company can be traced back to the recruitment stage. If you hire the wrong person you will have continuous problems. However, if you find someone who will fit into your culture you will avoid those problems. To do this, you have to define your desired culture.

My aim in creating the Employment Shield was to try to encompass, visually, those personal qualities which would enable someone to live the Groundrules. The qualities highlighted in the following subsections are not, of course, the only ones possessed by the particular image described, but they are the ones which I believe are most relevant to this aim. Assessing a potential employee against the Employment Shield allows you to select people who are able to thrive in the Thinking Organization, providing a blueprint that should run through everyone employed.

THE EMPLOYMENT SHIELD IMAGES

THE ANT

This tiny creature (of which, I am sad to say, I have killed many in my wicked, non-understanding, youth) is intriguing to me. Imagine this ...

It's the evening of a hot, summer's day. You've just had a barbecue and cleared up. As you are about to go indoors you look back. Because everything has been taken in, you are able to see small piles of food crumbs lying around. You also notice an ant, walking as if drunk on your alcoholic leftovers, in a zigzag fashion around the garden. Don't be tempted to stamp on it. Instead, watch for a while and see what happens.

This ant is a scout ant. Its job is to leave the nest and search for food. Its zigzag movement may look foolish but is actually quite efficient as it covers a wide area rather than a straight narrow 'corridor'.

Ah-ha! It has spotted some food, but seems to move on, almost uninterested. In fact, it has sent a message back to base saying 'Success – food found on co-ordinate numbers ...', before moving on to look for more.

Now the worker ants emerge, also, surprisingly, not walking in a straight line, because they are following the scent of the scout ant. However, if you watched for long enough you would see the line getting straighter as they collect the food and take it back to the nest. This is because the workers figure out that this is more efficient, given they only want to collect the food and go home. You now have a line of ants collecting and carrying a tremendous weight relative to their own, and the scout ant somewhere off in the distance, looking for more food.

But, what's this? All of a sudden the worker ants are being attacked by soldier ants from a nearby colony. Do the workers fight? No! They send a message back to base saying 'Help!'. Out come their own soldiers to engage the enemy and, for the purposes of this story, let's say they win. When they survey the damage the soldier ants tell the General ant, 'We lost 200 soldiers and 600 workers, but we battered the opposition'.

The General goes back to the Queen ant and fills in a requisition form, which the Queen reads. It goes something like this:

Dear Queen Ant

A fierce battle in which your soldiers were ultimately victorious, unfortunately resulted in some losses – namely, 200 soldiers and

600 workers. This requisition is therefore to cover replacement ants. We shall also need ten nursery staff and seven guards.

On a more positive note, with the death of the enemy soldiers we have enough food to keep the required newborns and their minders until they are ready to contribute to our glorious colony.

Yours gratefully and in 'Ant'icipation, etc., etc.

The Queen ant duly produces exactly what is required!

Employee qualities displayed by the ant

Strong, focused, having a total understanding of the role of others in the team, and persistent – who wouldn't want people with these qualities in their company?

THE KESTREL

Now you are a kestrel, hovering at about 100 feet alongside a motorway. You're thinking that it's cold, but it's good to be out of the nest, away from the moaning kids and the house lice that you don't seem to be able to get rid of.

Then you think, 'This is no good. I've got to shake these thoughts and get on with the "job in claw". I must find some food, otherwise I'll have to endure another nagging session from the "Beak Indoors" when I get home. ... Ah-ha! A lovely, big fieldmouse. Ger-on-i-mo!! Oh, shit, I missed! That hurt. And I think I've broken a nail ... twisted my ankle ... ouch ... have to hop. I hate this. Nothing going right – I think I read something about it in my stars last night. I'll probably get bloody run over now as well.'

Wake up! You're dreaming. ...

Employee qualities displayed by the kestrel

Of course, a kestrel would not be thinking like the one in the story. In fact, it hovers, seeing the whole picture before making its decision to dive. It focuses on its prey and moves positively to achieve its goal. And if it doesn't succeed, it just tries again. No fear of losing – persistence. Great qualities.

THE THINKER

Rodin's Thinker (1910) is such a success because it is clear what he is doing – thinking. And yet when you look at the Thinker with his athleticism and muscles, you would be forgiven for thinking he was a wrestler, pondering his next bout! The common perception of 'a thinker' has been a pallid, wet, weak, friendless nerd with thick-lensed spectacles. This needs changing! The dynamic and athletic Alexander the Great was a renowned great thinker, who had Aristotle as a teacher. And who could doubt the thinking skills of Leonardo da Vinci, Elizabeth I, Goethe and many more?

This sculpture, which portrays the seemingly invisible (the brain at work) has always been a favourite of mine and it should be no surprise to know that, in my office, I have a bronze copy of it.

I love the idea that Tony Buzan and Raymond Keene put forward in their book, *The Age Heresy* (1996), that the brain improves, rather than deteriorates, with age if continuously used.

Thinking is a wonderful exercise and disappearing with my own thoughts is one of my favourite pastimes. Rodin's Thinker, then, represents what I love to do – think. Furthermore, he looks like I want to look – but that's another story!

Employee qualities displayed by the Thinker

Although this sculpture evokes an immense range of imagery, my principal reason for placing the Thinker in my Shield was because he not only depicts continual conscious thinking, but also bodily fitness, athleticism and 'action' – key qualities of any employee in a Thinking Organization. I believe that he should, in one form or another, be displayed prominently in everyone's place of work.

THE LION

The lion conjures up a 'King of the Jungle' image – fearsome majesty, courage and power. As a company this is the image you want to project to your competitors. Interestingly, the lion himself is also perceived as being a 'great hunter', when in fact it is the lioness who hunts. I'm sure, therefore, as in other domestic circumstances, the female's view of the male might be different!

It is, however, the powerful 'King of the Jungle' image that earns him a place on my Shield and the courage, in particular, that I focus on. To do anything which is outside 'the norm' takes a great deal of courage. The easy way is to give up or follow convention.

Imagine that you have taken on new ideas or concepts and, on your return to work, all fired up, you try to implement them only to be put off or even put down by colleagues and managers saying dismissively, 'I can tell you've just been on a course ...' This is where extreme bravery is needed – particularly when you are in a minority of one.

Those who stand up for what they believe in will always achieve more than those who have no beliefs. Throughout history there have been numerous people who have achieved a great deal in the face of sceptics, and by their actions have advanced the whole human race. Examples would be Edison who was consistently told he was mad, Galileo who was told he was wrong and declared a heretic and Cézanne who was stoned in the street by those who thought his art was ridiculous.

Employee qualities displayed by the lion

Power beyond strength, leadership and charisma – all of which generate confidence. Those possessing these qualities are seen as powerful allies and supporters as well as formidable foes.

THE HANDS (PARTNERSHIP)

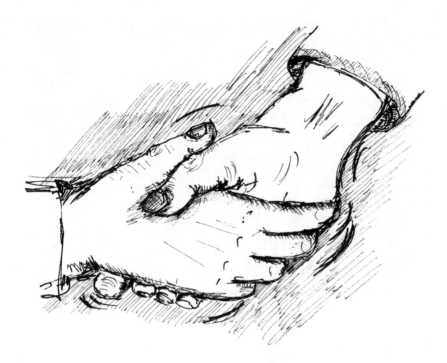

The joined hands symbolizing some of the qualities of someone who can live comfortably with the Groundrules, makes this image an obvious choice for the Shield. The whole point of the Groundrules is to get individual relationships right.

The hands symbolize an equal partnership. This does not mean doing away with hierarchy, or an atmosphere of permanent 'love and peace', it means making organizational structures work better. This can only be achieved if all parties feel equal in their ability to discuss their working relationships openly.

Hands also evoke an image of 'action'. Think of the ways in which we use our hands. I talk with mine. In fact, someone once said of me that if I had my hands cut off I would be speechless! We also mould, create, destroy, direct, explain, express and caress with our hands.

Employee qualities displayed by the hands

Cooperation, togetherness, partnership, understanding, visible belief in the common purpose.

WEALTH

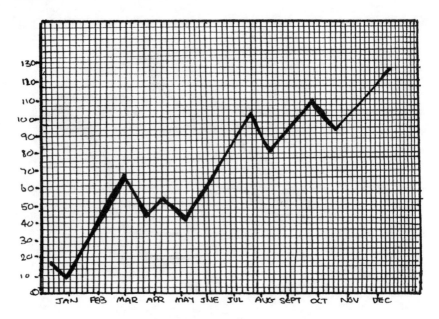

The wealth symbol brings to everyone's attention the fact that, without wealth, we do not have a company. This particular image also reinforces the idea of the company as a group of individuals. Not only does it symbolize 'corporate' wealth but can also be seen as depicting individual wealth facilitating many of our individual dreams (visions).

Equally, individual definitions of wealth can extend beyond the purely financial and encompass, for example, good health, spiritual health, the 'wealth of knowledge', a 'wealth of friends', a 'wealth of different experiences' and so on.

Employee qualities displayed by wealth

Dynamic achievers, with business understanding, positive resource managers with a pride in winning.

CAN DO!

'Can do' is the tag on the bottom of the Shield and is there to say that you will be valued if you have a 'can do' attitude. This is, as you know, one of the Groundrules so I will not elaborate on the power or effect of this phrase too much. Suffice to say that those who believe they can **probably will** and those who think they can't **definitely won't**.

Collectively the images of the Shield portray a person who is:

○	Ant	Strong
		Understands the team
○	Kestrel	Able to see the whole picture
		Focused
○	Thinker	Continuously thinking
		Athletic
		Action-oriented
○	Lion	Courageous
		Leader
		Charismatic
		Confident and confidence-inspiring
○	Hands	Cooperative
		Partnership-oriented
		Believes in common purpose (vision)
○	Wealth	Dynamic
		Winner
		Proud of achievements (of self and others)
○	Can Do	Positive

There are perhaps few people who possess all the qualities outlined, but identifying those qualities and striving to achieve them means that you will come much closer to the ideal than if you didn't try at all. Having a clear idea of the qualities you want also makes it possible to identify the gaps and begin to fill them.

FURTHER APPLICATIONS

Because the Groundrules are holistic they can apply in every area of the company. It is a question of looking at the system or process and asking 'How does this fit in with living the Groundrules?' Some examples are given below.

REWARD SYSTEM

'Reward' here implies any means of recognizing an employee – it could be by means of pay, benefits, promotion or gifts. Here the Groundrules are used to decide how those rewards are given. For instance, pay reviews could take into account how well the person lives the Groundrules.

Reward in terms of development or promotion can also be built around the Groundrules, thereby powerfully underlining that living the Groundrules is as important as – if not more important than – technical competence for success in your company.

TRAINING AND DEVELOPMENT

Perhaps one of the most common ways in which organizations waste money is on 'training and development'. They may spend significant amounts of time and money on 'courses' or other 'interventions' without realizing that, in many instances, 80 per cent of such training has disappeared within 24 hours of it taking place. The only effective way to train and develop the individuals which make up your organization is to create the right environment for that training and development to flourish.

This means knowing how people learn. It means teaching thinking (see Part II). It means understanding that real development involves changing behaviour and putting skills into practice and that, for this to happen, you need an environment in which employees are relaxed about identifying areas for improvement and confident about practising and developing these new skills.

Implementing the Groundrules creates this environment. This, in turn, means that investment in training and development generates real returns.

Using the Groundrules and understanding the characteristics shown on the Employment Shield makes it easier to analyse individual training needs. What might be preventing an employee from living the Groundrules? Lack of self-confidence might hinder **Honesty** or lack of time management skills might adversely effect an employee's preparedness and hence their **Professionalism**. Because the Groundrules focus on the individual they can be used to create individually-tailored training and development plans. Yet, the organization, as a whole, also benefits. Since each of the individual plans is aimed at helping the employee live the Groundrules more effectively there is a truly integrated approach. The result is genuine 'organization development'.

COMMUNICATION/CULTURE AUDITS AND ATTITUDE SURVEYS

It is easy to use the Groundrules as the basis for a questionnaire covering how employees feel that they are treated and to get their view of the company as an employer.

I used this initial 'temperature check' in BPFL during the early stages of implementing the Groundrules. At the time, the Directors were the only ones trying to live the Groundrules, and the survey was designed to find out how successful we were carrying this out. Although there were several areas which we still needed to work on, the results gave me sufficient confidence to start passing the Groundrules down to the next level of management.

The Groundrules can also be used in external relationships – for example, with the media and trade press. In fact a professional media person will already be familiar with an informal set of Groundrules ('off the record', 'on the record' and so on) and will appreciate the usefulness of a consistent approach to relationships.

SUPPLIER RELATIONSHIPS

The Groundrules can act as a very efficient audit of your supplier relationships.

This can be done by completing a review form for each supplier, or just the one about which you are concerned. Then, after explaining the process to your supplier(s), ask them to complete a review form on you.

This process, as with employees, draws out the key issues and allows you both to discuss them. You may be surprised to find out from the supplier that you are part of the problem! The exercise, in itself, will move your relationships forward simply because you have demonstrated a willingness to open up meaningful, two-way, discussions without becoming bogged down in tedious discussions of quality. Rather than holding a conversation centred round claims that 'This isn't up to specification,' drawing denials and justifications from the supplier, the approach is 'You caused me this problem in our relationship because this occurred – how do we stop this happening again?'

NEW SYSTEMS OR PROCESSES

When looking to change or introduce new computer systems or management control processes you can use the Groundrules to check that you are going in the right direction. For example, if you were implementing a new computer system, you would, as you know, begin with a 'specification'. If you are lucky, this will have been discussed during meetings with the users in advance. But how many users who attend such meetings completely understand the consequences of their discussions? If you simply apply the decision you are about to make to the Groundrules and check that it does not significantly breach them, you will almost certainly arrive at the right course of action. By so doing, you focus discussion on how the system will affect your business relationships when it is in use rather than being driven solely by technical considerations.

DECISION-MAKING

 I was recently talking to an exasperated Chairman who had discovered that one of the staff in his company had ordered a particular product in such bulk quantities that storage had become a problem – as had cashflow. He wondered how the Groundrules could have stopped this kind of mistake happening. Easy!

First, employees do not come into work to fail. In this instance it turned out the employee had ordered in this quantity because of the discounts available on bulk purchase. If that individual had been able to apply the decision to the Groundrules I believe the following would have happened.

O **Improvement**. This action would not help company performance in that it would tie up borrowed capital on which interest is being paid. (I imagine that the employee never considered this issue and probably genuinely thought that they were improving the company's performance by buying more cheaply.)

O **Ownership**. Would the employee really spend their own money in this way?

O **Understanding**. I'm not sure that anyone else in the organization (for example, finance, warehousing) was even considered – yet they clearly should have been.

O **Can Do**. The employee did well here.

O **Honesty**. This was not relevant to this decision.

○   **Availability**. Again, this was not relevant to this decision.

○   **Professionalism**. Attention to detail was clearly a problem as was knowledge of the subject, since a purchaser should be aware of the financial implications of decisions taken.

In handling any situation similar to that related above, the solution is not to remove the authority for making such decisions from the employee. Although this is often the action taken, it does not help the employee make better decisions in the future. They remain passive in the real decision-making process.

The answer is to explain, against the Groundrules, why the decision caused a problem and how to judge future decisions against the Groundrules framework as well as against other business criteria, such as financial authority. This approach identifies gaps and, if nothing else, convinces others of technical or process shortfalls.

VISION AND MISSION AUDIT

It is easy to identify potential flaws and problems simply by applying the Groundrules to a vision and mission. The advantage this gives is twofold. First, you can choose to adjust the vision or mission accordingly. Second, if you have decided that neither are to change then you are well placed to think through, in advance, how you are going to handle the potential problem you've identified.

Example

Imagine that you wanted to assess your vision and mission against the following Groundrule.

Improvement

All individuals and groups of individuals are seen to be **continuously** seeking to **improve relationships**, **processes**, **themselves** and the **company's performance**.

Subword: 'continuously'   I would hope that your vision and mission are seen as continuous at the outset, so there should be no problem here.

Subwords: 'improve relationships'   Your new vision and mission may upset some relationships because:

○   You will be demanding more.

○ You will be tougher with customers – for example, you may decide to improve profitability by firming up profit margins.
○ You may have decided to launch a hostile bid for a competitor.

Subwords: 'improve processes'   In the short term, processes needed to achieve your vision and mission may be interrupted by:

○ a new computer system
○ a reduction in staff
○ moving your offices, distribution facilities, factory and so on.

Subwords: 'improve themselves'   Your new vision and mission may need so much work that you interrupt the process of your staff self-development programme.

Subwords: 'improve the company's performance'   In the short term, due to restructuring, major investment and so forth, you may seem to be pushing the company backwards or, at best, sideways.

If any of the potential problems or issues outlined above were true, and further issues emerged as a result of applying the remaining Groundrules, then you could begin to consider, sufficiently far in advance, what, if anything, you could do to overcome some or all of them.

PERSONAL

The Groundrules can be applied, as outlined above, to your personal life in areas such as:

○ family relationships
○ community relationships
○ stress management
○ personal (life) audits
○ career management, planning and development.

SUMMARY

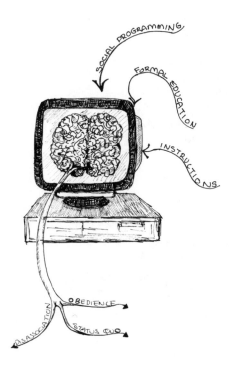

Without Groundrules

Analogies have often been made between linking the brain with a
computer. The illustration above is a representation of what exists
prior to the introduction of the Groundrules. The computer (brain)

software is social programming, formal education and instruction. The result is obedience (hopefully), status quo (average) and disassociation from actions.

VISION

Your vision must be:

- **powerful**
- **dynamic**
- **short**
- **easy to remember**
- **visual**
- **achievable**.

MISSION

Your mission should:

- **state strategy**
- **be visual and brief**
- **be easy to remember**
- **be achievable**.

GROUNDRULES

The Groundrules are:

- **easy to remember**
- **lived by all**
- **based on individual relationships**
- **holistic** and
- **regularly reviewed**

The resulting environment will:

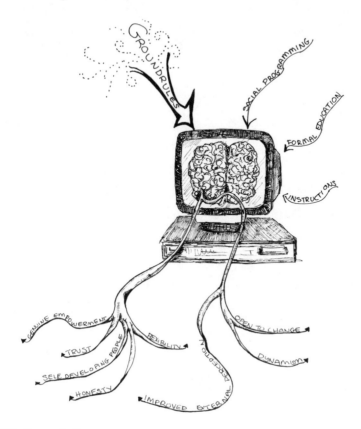

With Groundrules

With the addition of the Groundrules 'software', the results are dramatically different from the previous illustration.

- O   **create total focus on achieving the vision**
- O   **be relationship-driven and supported by systems and processes**
- O   **be dynamic (based on 'yes' (can do))**
- O   **have controls self-generated by employees empowered through the Groundrules framework**
- O   **develop and value individualism.**

ACTION PLAN

 Before you move on to Part II, consider the following questions:

1 **Do I have a vision?**
If 'yes', is it clear enough?
If 'no', you must create one. How can decisions be made if the decision-maker doesn't know to what end the decision is driving?

2 **Do I have a mission?**
If 'yes', is it just a statement of what you do? Is it genuinely useful in terms of helping people decide what they must do to achieve the vision?
If 'no', create one. Don't be afraid to use outside help in creating a mission. A good facilitator working with a team can make short work of this issue.

3 **Do I have the correct environment for winning?**
If 'yes' could the Groundrules help you communicate that you do?
If 'no', you need the Groundrules quickly. The effect of introducing the Groundrules at the top management level will quickly be noticed by the rest of the organization. Don't be tempted to rush the process and introduce the concept to everyone immediately. Unless top management lives by the Groundrules and fully understand their interpretations they will not work lower down the organization. Lead by example.

4   **Check yourself against the Groundrules.**
        You need to live by the Groundrules in order to teach them. Each
        Sunday evening whilst relaxing before bed I mentally measure my
        relationship performance from the previous week against the
        Groundrules. It is not always good, and this exercise helps me
        reflect on what I could have done better. The result of my
        reflections is inevitably a better week ahead.

REVIEW BY TONY BUZAN

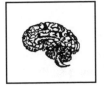

I'm sure my friend Rikki, and you, the reader, will be delighted to know that the three fundamental tools he has discovered are in direct alignment with the great success stories of the human race.

VISION

The human brain is, by design, a vision-seeking machine. Virtually our whole life is a series of visions followed by appropriate (and sometimes inappropriate!) actions. It is easiest to see this in day-to-day activities. The simple act of drinking a glass of water is preceded by a vision of what is wanted, the vision of its location and the 'soft vision' of the successful completion of the desired goal.

Mentally review a standard day in your normal life, and count the number of times you 'vision' before acting. Estimate the percentage of successful completions, and you will realize that you are an ongoing success story!

The great leaders, great organizations, great nations and empires took this ability of the human brain to its logical extreme, creating gigantic visions which they then followed to conclusions. Additional examples to those already given in the book, and which you may wish to compare with your own, include those of Alexander the Great whose simple vision was 'to know everything; to see everything; to conquer everything'. Thomas Edison's vision was not simply to invent the lightbulb: it was much grander – 'to light the Planet Earth at night'. Muhammed Ali, often considered as the greatest heavyweight boxer ever, had one overriding goal, not suprisingly, to be 'the Greatest'. It is also interesting to note that, in the earliest part of the twentieth century, Thomas Watson, who was to found the largest company in the history of commerce, had insisted that all his employees at IBM should have in their professional life one prime goal, summarized by the word that he insisted they all place on their desks: 'Think'.

MISSION

The most successful people throughout human history have always backed up their vision with a mission which included the following principal thinking areas:

O   short-term planning
O   mid-term planning
O   long-term planning
O   analytical thinking
O   strategic thinking
O   creative/flexible thinking.

Looking at this list it becomes blazingly apparent that it is not only desirable to train everyone in an organization in these thinking skills, it is **essential**.

THE GROUNDRULES

The Groundrules, under the acronym IOUCHAP, are a proven formula. It is instructive to consider them from a brain and mind–body perspective.

IMPROVEMENT

The human brain is a success mechanism – it is designed to succeed. As evidence of the delicate nature of this necessary evolutionary imperative, educational experiments designed to explore the Pygmalion (*My Fair Lady*) effect produced dramatic results. When children were assumed to be bright and well mannered they tended increasingly to become so; when similar children were considered dull and delinquent they likewise grew to fit the mould of the vision that others had of them. In other words expectation (the vision) has a significant impact and influence on performance (action).

An organization which perceives its personnel as continuously improving in terms of their relationships, processes, self-development and the company's performance will dramatically improve its probability of reaching its goals.

A happy correlative of this is that when people are successful, **all** their systems improve: poise and posture become more erect and aligned; breathing is deeper and more rhythmical; the heartbeat is slower; blood pressure is reduced; circulation is improved; muscular tension is released; and general stress levels are reduced.

Put simply, the individual becomes far more healthy. As such, they are more wealthy. So it will be with the Thinking Organization.

OWNERSHIP

One of the foundation stones for memory, creativity and thinking is the process of association which is a facilitator, stimulator and prime motivator. When the brain can make the correct association it **remembers**. When the brain can make the appropriate association it **understands**. When the brain can make a new association it **creates**.

Ownership is an important form of association. When someone claims 'ownership' of something, **they follow up with action**. They take up a hobby, buy a pet, establish a family or buy a product or service.

The Thinking Organization in which all employees 'own the company', will have a workforce that is truly motivated and empowered.

UNDERSTANDING

Brain research during the last decade of the twentieth century has shown the human brain to have a hundred times more capacity than had previously been believed.

Any organization which recognizes this fact and makes full use of the extraordinary potential of each individual's brain, is tapping into a 'goldmine'.

'CAN DO' APPROACH

Once again, referring to the geniuses of history, the records show that, even when faced by the greatest adversity and plunged into the deepest depressions they remained fundamentally and unremittingly positive in their approach. Their vision was so strong, their commitment so absolute that nothing would stop them. This approach led them to confound the apparent contradiction between having an absolute goal whilst being infinitely creative. They used their 'can do' approach to pass through, around, under or over whatever obstacle was impeding their progress towards their goal. In other words, they displayed the ultimate creativity.

Unleashing such creativity guarantees the Thinking Organization unassailable advantages in the competitive business environment.

HONESTY

Investigations into the nature of the brain's fundamental mechanisms have revealed that it is, not only a success-directed but also a truth-seeking mechanism. Why? Quite simply, for the purposes of survival. If we do not know the truth of the relationship between a three-ton lorry heading towards us and our body, it will be the final interesting event of our lives!

Similarly, if we do not know the 'single truth' of our relationships with other people, our survival is threatened. Regardless of the moral or ethical considerations, the fact is that if you lie to someone you simply reduce their chances of survival. An organization with honesty at its core is going to be a tougher competitor in the evolutionary race.

AVAILABILITY

From the 'business brain's' point of view, availability simply means that the important channels of communication are open. This perfectly reflects the internal structures and mechanisms of the brain itself: your million million brain cells are designed as 'open-channel communicators' instantaneously allowing any important information to pass through, directing it to where it is of the most use for your needs.

Being open and available has profound implications for the leader. When the system is open, everything flows smoothly and rapidly and, coincidentally, all five senses become more alert and focused. Conversely, when information and communication channels are blocked, action necessarily becomes 'treading water', rather than striking out towards the goal; all the senses become relatively 'blurred' because they have nothing on which to focus; time becomes compoundly wasted; and most importantly, that ultimately vital tool, thinking, becomes directed away from the vision and mission and towards building giant and unnecessary thought patterns around the multiple questions (many of them negative and ultimately irrelevant) around the failure of the leader to communicate.

From the 'business brain's' point of view, the question of 'availability' or 'non-availability' is a no-brainer! Availability *must* rule!

PROFESSIONALISM

Showing attention to detail, being well prepared, having extensive knowledge in your subject area, and being focused on the goal are attributes, like those discussed under 'Mission', which incorporate a number of the different qualities of the great historical geniuses and leaders. They include: short-, mid- and long-term planning, subject knowledge, truth and honesty, and a passionate love of the task.

As you might expect, each of these skills complements and enhances the others. The brain has planned from the immediate present to the long-term future, has a clear route-map and will not waste valuable time stumbling around in unnecessary (to the goal) territory.

Because great geniuses and leaders were so passionately in love with their subject areas they automatically acquired vast amount of knowledge. This helped them both to plan and gain respect from their followers. Outstanding leaders such as Alexander the Great, Andrew Carnegie, Goethe, Queen Elizabeth I and Thomas Jefferson used to astound their followers with the depth and breadth of their knowledge. At the same time, they would also consistently surprise them by admitting to areas of ignorance. They had become aware of the ancient proverb that the more you know the more you become aware of what there is to know and therefore of the vast area of your own ignorance.

To the great leader ignorance is seen not as a shameful quality that needs to be hidden and disguised, but as a vast and limitless opportunity to acquire new knowledge and experience. All great brains and great leaders were like 'Columbuses of Thought', setting out with courage, vision and a childlike enthusiasm to discover new continents of knowledge, creativity and thinking.

In addition to these aforementioned advantages, professionalism imbues the individual with a growing confidence that feeds back on itself in a positive and inspiring loop. Increased confidence increases the ability to plan, acquire knowledge, focus and lead, which in turn leads to an even greater professionalism and so on into a happy infinity!

PART II
THINKING IN THE ENVIRONMENT

❖

INTRODUCTION TO PART II

 Part II looks at all aspects of 'thinking' in the environment that you, through the Groundrules, will have created.

Chapter 5 explores some facts about the brain, including the key fact that most of what we know today about the brain has been discovered in the last 20 years or so! Physical fitness and its impact on the brain is covered, as well as the effects and importance of diet, drugs, sleep, rest and sex on this, our most under used organ! Also considered is mental attitude and its obvious effects, as well as mental challenge and mental stimuli.

In Chapter 6 'thinking' is defined, as distinct from 'learning'. It is proposed that, before you can attempt to create a 'learning organization', you must first create a Thinking Organization. Real examples are given to show how **changing the way you think will change the way you act**. This point is pivotal to understanding the Thinking Organization.

The chapter also considers how much time each day, week, year, should be dedicated to thinking. If scientific research is based on observation, analysis and evaluation, then the view put forward here comes close to scientific study – based, as it is, on years of observing what actually happens and the results generated. Clearly, one of the main drivers is the recognition that thinking without action achieves either little or nothing.

Chapter 7 explores dynamic ways of thinking. You may have heard it said that the brain is like a computer, only more powerful, but what does this statement actually mean? Consider it this way:

O   The physical brain is the hardware.
O   Our experiences (good and bad) are the computer's programming.

O   Our learning (technical and cerebral) are our software packages.

The teaching of thinking is the key software because it is designed to help us:

O   make sense of the programming we have received
O   make sense of the learning we have received
O   decide what we are going to do about this.

EXAMPLE: PROGRAMMING VERSUS THINKING SOFTWARE

If a five-year-old runs across a busy road and *just* gets away with it, the parents will act in a 'programming' way. One example of programming would be a mother, seeing one of her children do this, saying 'I'll kill you if you do that again'!

This approach programmes the child not to do it again and so achieves a specific objective. But it does not help the child think through *why* they should not do it and then apply that thinking to other potentially life-threatening situations.

The point is not how you should deal with a five-year-old in this situation but to illustrate that, if we were taught thinking, we would be much better users of reason. There is a conscious link in our minds between what we do and who made the decision to do it. If we, ourselves, make the decision, based on considered thought, we take more responsibility for our actions.

I'm sure most people would agree that the best – and certainly the most creative – thinkers are children. It seems ironic that we are born geniuses, then taught that we are idiots and spend a lifetime trying to get back to our starting point!

Thinking techniques should be taught to, and in, all schools. They should also be made available to parents and all others involved in education. One hour a week would have a profound effect on efficiency as well as ability. By teaching two hours of thinking as the first lesson each week, or even 15 minutes each morning, the brain would be 'put into gear', would learn more quickly and more effectively – saving three times that time investment later in the week.

From the moment of birth we begin the process of social programming. Everything learnt in these early stages is learned by copying – good examples being walking and speaking. Indeed, how many of us have been embarrassed by our children loudly showing off words copied 'from Daddy' which we would rather they didn't! We soak up, like sponges, the culture or attitudes of those around us. Our own character then begins to put an individual spin on what we are receiving and as we come into contact with more and more people, our programming becomes based on a wider spectrum. At this stage, we also become more selective about what we will accept into our personal programme.

An example may be programming by our parents that 'helping others is a good thing'. Our peers may think that this is not true. This gives us two viewpoints from which to choose. Whichever attitude we decide to adopt, we also add our own thoughts and, in this way, we take ownership of our decision. Sometimes the programming we receive and accept is 'bad'. It is at this stage that we may feel confused.

Suppose you could add a brilliant piece of software which would give you more chance of success in selecting the correct route! Well you can. You can add the Groundrules software. This will give you a good grounding in social behaviour – relating to people. You can then add the 'thinking techniques' software. These, together, will help you open up more options when faced with a difficult decision.

The output from these three pieces of input data (social programming, Groundrules and thinking techniques) will be people who can analyse why they are the type of person they are and match this against the Groundrules to produce more socially skilled human beings with a hunger for continuous learning.

 When my son's school report stated that he does not concentrate as much as he should, I smiled. I used to go on some wonderful journeys while, in reality, rooted to my school chair! Whilst the majority of schools do not currently teach thinking techniques, this does not mean that you cannot. Here is a game of thinking that I play with my sons on the way to school. The goal is simply to get their brains into gear.

This game can be played anywhere, anytime and can last five minutes or two hours. It is a particularly useful exercise on the way to school as it has the effect of 'switching the brain on'. I call it 'Tell me a story about ...' and it's based on 'I spy'. My son begins by saying 'Tell me a story about...' and then looks around and selects an object he can see – say, 'a truck wheel' (or something easier if I'm lucky!). I then have to make up a story which may go like this ...

One day there was a truck wheel who was not happy. He said to his mate, on the other side of the truck, 'I'm not happy. The fool driving this truck is getting on my tread! He's driving so badly that he has to keep braking really hard and, quite frankly, my bum's burnt!'

The truck pulls into a café and the two wheels continue their discussion. They decide to get their own back. At a point when the truck is doing 50 mph they both look for something in the road. One of them spots a clump of wood, shouts to the other (because it's noisy) and they pull hard together, forcing the truck on to the wood. The driver loses control and, as a result, the load falls off the back of the truck. This causes chaos on the road. No one is injured, but that's because the wheels planned it that way. The driver, however, is severely reprimanded by his boss and never drove badly again.

I could, of course, continue the story (and sometimes do). Then I select an object and ask one of my sons to tell a story. Doing this on the way to school puts all our brains into gear, helps our relationships and boosts our creative skills.

Recently I met an old school friend. One of his first questions was 'What happened?'. He wanted to know what had changed me from what I was – a quiet, unconfident individual – to what I am now (a very successful leader, according to him). On considering the question, I concluded that there were a number of principles that govern my own thinking and, as a result, my actions:

1   **I have never accepted that what I am is what I am going to be**. That's defeatist. It also makes no sense from a pure survival point of view. I prefer to control the way I change rather than have circumstances dictate it.

2   I have always believed that **I can learn more**. You think with what you know. **The more you put into your brain the more options it can create**.

3   **I have practised, and am committed to practising, what I learn**. This is where I part company with most other people. I find that many people who go on courses or read books find it difficult to make the progression from head-nodding to practice, probably because of fear (of failure itself, ridicule, change and so on).

4   **I want new experiences and use them to gain knowledge so that I can grow**. I have no fear of allowing others to do the same and derive pleasure from seeing this happen.

5   **I have an absolute belief that people are basically good**. I don't know of anyone who wakes up and thinks 'How can I screw my company?'.

6   **I believe that there is much untapped ability in the world**. Success in any organizations is only brought about through its people. If you think that you can achieve through others without a genuine belief in people you're wrong – your attitude will become obvious to others within five minutes and you will lose. To get the most from this book you must genuinely believe that

people are the key and that creating an environment which facilitates the teaching of thinking is one of the most important ways of helping people reach their potential.

7   **I believe in individuality** (this belief is fundamental to the Groundrule model). We are all different and people will feel less threatened if their organization recognizes this. It also leads to greater communication and better results. We should all be mavericks!

8   As far as individual growth is concerned, **I do not find the concept of 'success' or 'failure' particularly helpful. I prefer 'winning' and 'losing'**. This allows me to cope better with my 'loss'. Instead of seeing 'failure' I see gained experiences. **I consider losing as part of the elimination process in the race to win**.

Chapter 7 on thinking techniques gives real examples which show how a combination of techniques was used to create a long-term plan. Explanations have been simplified wherever possible.

It is for you to decide which techniques to learn or teach. However, because we are all individual and therefore respond individually to each issue confronting us, you must learn or teach several techniques. Learning or teaching several techniques allows for choice. You can experiment and find two or three which work best for you and/or your organization.

Part II, then, shows you how to make use of your newly created environment by applying thinking techniques. It concludes with a summary, an action plan and another review by Tony Buzan.

5

USING YOUR BRAIN

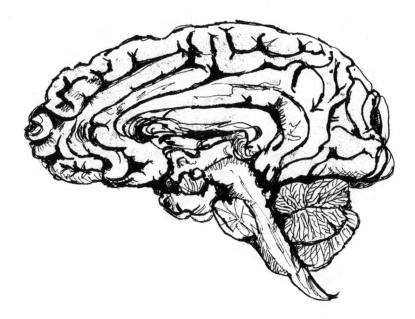

As long as you recognise the picture above as something you carry with you on most – if not all – occasions, you have the raw material to be able to think!

Most of us don't realize that, in our 'Adonis'- or 'Venus'-like bodies (now there's an example of creative thinking on my part!), we carry the equivalent of the most powerful computer known to man, multiplied by 10 000 million.

Consider the number of security precautions surrounding one of NASA's computers. Yet we often leave ours behind, forget to switch it on and fail to even carry out a basic maintenance programme! As we travel from country to country, we are, in effect, smuggling in a huge piece of equipment without paying any import tax! Perhaps next time you go through Customs, you should stand in the 'something to declare' queue. When you get to the front, instead of putting your suitcase on the table, put your head on it and say 'How much for this, mate?'. Of course, I can't be responsible for the outcome, but you see my point. ...

Most of us know less about our brain than we do about fully utilizing all the software programs on our laptops – and few know much about that! The reason for our lack of knowledge about the brain is twofold. First, most scientific research on the brain has been carried out over the last ten to 20 years.

So, in 1962 – the year Decca rejected the Beatles ('they'll never make it in the Charts'), John Glenn became the first American to orbit the earth, Bonington and Clough became the first Britons to conquer the north face of the Eiger, the first hovercraft entered service between Rhyl and Wallasey – we didn't possess a tenth of the knowledge about how the brain was used to achieve some of these feats.

Furthermore, even when we did discover that the brain was something that we could grow and train, no-one in school told us. What is more frightening is that, today, now we do have the knowledge, we are still not teaching students, *en masse*, how to use it.

SOME FACTS ABOUT THE BRAIN

○   The brain contains approximately 1 billion cells – that is, equivalent to 150 times the population of the planet. Put another way, you are carrying 150 planets in your head, each with the same brain cell population as planet Earth's people population!

○   Each single brain cell has the capacity to make between 10 000 and 100 000 connections.

○   Each single brain cell has the genetic capacity to reproduce the whole person!

○   In the 1970s we believed that we only used 50 per cent of our brain's capacity. By the 1980s this had been revised to 10 per cent and, by the 1990s, it was accepted that we use less than 1 per cent.

○   The brain's effectiveness increases the more it is used.

HOW TO KEEP THE BRAIN FIT FOR ACTION

You are no doubt familiar with many exercises designed to keep the body fit. But do you know how to keep your brain fit?

The Greeks and Romans practised the principle of 'healthy body, healthy mind'. In fact, many geniuses were also, in today's terms, 'fitness freaks'. Leonardo da Vinci, for example, was known as the strongest man in Florence.

As with anything on the planet, from cars to forests, we can choose to use or abuse our brains. If driven carefully and well maintained, cars will last much longer than those that are not. Forests that are nurtured and managed (as opposed to interfered with) will flourish. The same is true of the brain. Love it, feed it, exercise it and it will serve you well. However, make sure that you understand what you're doing. You can do more harm than good by trying some technique designed to help your brain if you do not really know what it is meant to achieve because, if you do not get instant success, you may give up and never try again.

My Dad was one of the great army of 'tinkerers'. It seemed to me that every Sunday was 'tinkering Sunday', much in the way that every Saturday was 'football Saturday'.

As a child, I paid little attention to what day it was. Of course, the weekend was special because I had no need to play truant from school. I always knew, however, when it was Sunday. Not because we all went to church, not because we had a Sunday roast, but because, all along our street, you could see cars and vans with their bonnets up and hear the muffled sound of swearing coming from underneath.

When my Dad tinkered, the van inevitably suffered. Having caused a problem, he would look to me and say 'It's me tappetts'. For years I thought he was ill!

PHYSICAL FITNESS

Although many of us try to keep relatively physically fit, few of us – even 'fitness freaks' and athletes – also concentrate on mental fitness. It is difficult to attain mental fitness in a rundown body – rather like putting a brand new engine in a car held together by Sellotape.

Now, I'm no Arnie Schwarzenegger or Sylvester Stallone. I'm more like your Marlon Brando, prone to the odd weight problem. So I have to work at my physical fitness. Like most people, I occasionally lapse, but the fact that I know what I should be doing encourages me to keep trying. For example, I know that aerobic exercise is best for the brain because it provides more oxygen which is, of course, good brain food.

I like to row and use a step machine, as well as run. My ideal is about 45 minutes, three times a week, allocated as follows:

- ○   5 minutes warm-up – body stretches, arm circling and hip twisting
- ○   10 minutes rowing on a Concept II rowing machine
- ○   10 minutes on the step machine (on toes to strengthen calves)
- ○   10 minutes back on the rowing machine and finally
- ○   10 more minutes on the step machine (this time, on heels to strengthen hamstrings and thighs)
- ○   5 minutes cool-down session – leisurely stretching.

I use a pace watch and try to keep my heart at between 140 and 160 beats per minute. Your maximum heart rate is calculated by subtracting your age from 210 – for example, I am 45, so my maximum would be 165.

DIET

Diet is also important for the functioning of the brain, but here I really do struggle. What I should be doing is eating predominantly fresh – as opposed to processed – food and varying the content of my meals, because constantly eating the same food can clog up the system or cause you to miss out on some vital element. Being a vegetarian, and a busy one at that, I tend to eat ready-prepared meals and pizzas. But, because I do notice an amazing difference if I eat freshly cooked meals, I'm trying to improve my habits. I also feel much better if I eat breakfast (in my case, cereal and/or an apple), especially mid-morning – I suppose an engine tends to stop when it runs out of fuel!

DRUGS

Hopefully, you are aware of the dangers of the most obviously damaging drugs – heroin, Ecstasy and the like – whose side-effects include memory loss, neurological damage, depression and even death. But we shouldn't forget the most widely used drugs – tobacco and alcohol – both of which do have an effect on the brain and body.

I have to admit to liking a drink, although I don't smoke.

SLEEP AND REST

Your brain needs regular breaks, as well as regular activity. We can all think of instances when the brain has told us to rest. For me, this has often occurred while writing this book. At times I have hit a brick wall. Usually a short break and some more fuel is enough to set me back to work.

SEX

Your biggest sex organ is not between the legs (that's a relief!) but between the ears. The brain is your largest erogenous zone.

Apart from being fun, (safe) sex is one of the greatest all-round exercises. It builds stamina, helps flexibility, improves your skin and provides an excellent cardiovascular workout.

Sex is also a great stress reliever and promotes, relaxation, as well as being good for fitness – it is the ultimate panacea.

MENTAL ATTITUDE

Having the correct mental attitude can only help us in all we do. I'm sure most, if not all, of us can recall occasions when we have felt 'mentally drained'.

Studies carried out by the British America Association and the American Medical Association have shown that as much as 80 per cent of disease is caused by mental attitude.

One of the most striking characteristics of a fit and healthy 70-year-old is their positive outlook on life.

'If you think you will lose, you will. If you think you will win, you may.' The chasm between these two attitudes is immense.

While climbing Mont Blanc I became ill 1000 metres from the summit (and that's a long way when you're looking up). I had a chest infection, which was giving me a bad cough, I'd lost toenails due to wearing ill fitting boots, I had osteoarthritis in my knees, (as I later found out) and was suffering the effects of a short fall down a glacier! Observing my sorry plight, David Hempleman-Adams OBE, one of my companions on the trip, assured me, 'Rikki, to turn back now wouldn't be a disgrace. This is your first climb and you're at 3800 metres. It took me three attempts to climb this mountain.'

I lifted my chin off my chest and said 'If you're looking for a cop-out, it's not going to be me.'

David Hempleman-Adams, OBE, explorer *extraordinaire* (seven summits, five of the six poles, first to hot air balloon over the Andes and so on) told me afterwards, 'Your body was clapped out; it was only your head that got you there.'

UNLOCKING THE BRAIN'S POTENTIAL

Knowing how to keep the brain physically fit – to prepare it for action – is a start, but we also need to know how to keep it working and developing.

Mental fitness falls into two areas: **mental challenge** – for example, overcoming fears – and **mental stimulus** – that is, adding data, knowledge, experience and so forth to your brain.

MENTAL CHALLENGE

Constantly challenging yourself is a sure route to continuous improvement. I recently challenged myself to ski (as a complete non-skier) to the magnetic North Pole.

Setting out to achieve my goal challenged more than just my physical fitness and my mental attitude. The whole venture challenged how I thought about everything. You have a great deal of time to think when you are in the middle of nowhere.

Mental challenge is vital if we want to grow. Constantly challenging ourselves to face our fears can only be beneficial. Some examples of typical fears are the easily recognizable fear of heights, spiders, sailing, flying and so on, all of which are personal phobias. Whatever your fear, or phobia, from time to time, consider the benefits of beating it. You really do feel like a million dollars when you overcome it. On Mont Blanc I was continually fearful – before that the highest I'd climbed was to the top of our stairs, and if I did that quickly I became dizzy! Now, I could climb Mount Everest and, by 2005, I intend to.

MENTAL STIMULUS

Mental stimulus is the real 'brain food' of cerebral growth. If we accept that we make decisions or 'think' using our knowledge, intuition and desires, then it follows that the better the knowledge base, the better the decision. This means that we need to keep adding information, from whatever source we can. We must read, listen and observe. We think with what we know. If you limit what you know you will limit your potential.

The Thinking Organization plays a vital role in helping its people progress in the areas of mental challenge (by concentrating on removing fear of change and failure), mental stimulus (by encouraging the acquisition of as much knowledge as possible) and by teaching thinking techniques

CONCLUSION

Having learnt a little more about the brain, understood how to look after it and discovered that everyone can increase their mental capacity it is now time to examine a definition of 'thinking' and distinguish it from 'learning'.

6

THINKING ABOUT THINKING

THINKING VERSUS LEARNING

Two of the latest 'buzz words' are 'intellectual property' and 'knowledge-based organizations'. Both of these are of little use without the capacity to think. As Tony Buzan has recently commented, 'the twenty-first century will be the century of the brain', adding that 'thinking will be one of its 'prime foci'.

In the 'Introducing the Authors' I mentioned how I disliked school. This was because I did not enjoy the learning process. Day in day out, I was lectured to and expected to understand and memorize. Many people can, of course, learn in this way and do gain a great deal from lectures. But I didn't on account of the fact that I tend to be a very 'visual' and 'feeling' person. As a result, my most vivid memory from school is visual – of a teacher, portraying one of Chaucer's *Tales* by having a member of the class dress as a skeleton who had come back to haunt. And, interestingly, when, recently, on the school's fortieth anniversary, I relayed the story to others, they all remembered the incident and who the skeleton was!

It would be easy to say that a Thinking Organization is a follow-on from a learning organization. But I have a problem with this! I only learn if I think about what is being said. If I don't think about what is said then I am merely memorizing information. This is a useful skill but, to progress, I have to think for myself. It follows therefore that a learning organization cannot succeed unless it is first a Thinking Organization.

By learning we acquire information. By thinking we interpret today's learning and create tomorrow's learning.

The thesaurus lists the following synonyms, which further help explain the difference.

○   **thinking**
  – **cerebrating**: deliberating, meditating, reasoning, reflecting, speculating
  – **thoughtful**: contemplative, meditative, pondering
  – **conceiving**: envisioning, imagining, prospecting, visualizing
  – **understanding:** idea, opinion, conceiving, believing
○   **learning**
  – **education**: known facts, ideas and skills that have been imparted
  – **discovering**: catching on, finding out, hearing, seeing
  – **'getting'**: mastering or picking up
  – **memorizing**: remembering (what you have been told)

It is no coincidence that so many of the thinking synonyms are to do with 'seeing', or imagining – they are to do with the future. Developing skills that take you into the future are key for any organization or individual. You will also see the link here between the emphasis on **taking responsibility for the future** (that is, having thinking skills) and the role of the leader outlined later.

A prerequisite for any change in behaviour is a change in thinking. If you don't think about and understand why you need to change you won't. **Change the way you think and you will change the way you act.**

EXAMPLE: HOW CHANGING THINKING CHANGES ACTIONS

On my second day in BPFL while I was working late, I became bored and was considering going home when I remembered that I had been invited to go to a pre-season friendly football match between the local team, Swindon Town, and Real Sociedad.

As a lifetime Liverpool fan and having been brought up on the likes of Roger Hunt, Ian St John, Tommy Smith, Ian Callahan, Kenny

Continued

Dalgleish and Kevin Keegan I could see no sense in going to watch what was, to me, the equivalent of a Northern Sunday League match.

However, there I was, in Swindon and wasn't Glen Hoddle the club's new manager? Also John Toshack, an ex-Liverpool player, was manager of Real Sociedad and (the *pièce de résistance*) John Aldridge, (also ex-Liverpool) was playing for them!

I remember that there were 5000 or so people in the stadium which held 15–20 000. Along with the Mayor of Swindon I was told that seating was not an issue; we should ignore our ticket numbers and sit where we liked, which we did. Just before kick-off a Swindon fan came and asked me to move because I was in his seat. I explained what I had been told and pointed out that he had plenty of seats to choose from as half the stand was empty. He replied rather aggressively, 'I'm a season ticket holder and I paid £300 for that seat.' My response, which I knew would annoy him, was 'Why – you could have bought something good for £300!'.

Worse was to come. John Aldridge had been transferred to Tranmere Rovers the day before and would not be playing!

Despite all the above, I became involved with Swindon Town Football Club as their principal sponsor, and it was extremely successful in raising brand awareness for my company at a time when we were changing brand design. I was later asked to join the Board on the basis that some 'big business' skill would be useful to them.

When I first became a Director I would go along to the club, sit in my Board seat and watch the match. I would clap politely when Swindon were doing well and occasionally became rather agitated when the referee or linesman made a decision with which I disagreed. Basically, I was reacting as somebody connected with the club but not as a fan. Over time, of course, I became more involved with the club. I got to know the players, the manager, the Directors and the fans and to see me now in the stand you would think I'd been born and bred in Swindon colours!

I changed the way I thought about the club because I was exposed to it in a different way and began to want all those involved to win. This change in my thinking drove the change in the way I acted.

Once during an away game I became so incensed by a particular decision that, at half-time, I was approached by the away club Chairman and told that the police cameras had caught me offering to take on 28 000 home fans! Pointing out that this sort of behaviour was imprudent at best, he suggested that I watched the rest of the match on TV in the Director's room. About ten minutes into the second half, he returned to the suite and told me that, although it was true I'd been picked up on camera, he had in fact vouched for my good character and was only joking that I should be confined to the suite! I had clearly changed how I thought about Swindon Town Football Club, and this had translated into changed actions – for the better and for life.

Clearly, to be at our most effective in terms of the actions we take we need to be able to think and to learn. As discussed in the 'Introduction' to Part II, we must begin to teach thinking in our schools. We must create an interest and awareness of our prime asset – our brain. Our education would be more complete and our learning more effective if we knew *how* to think. Teaching thinking also empowers ownership of our actions, helping us think through the consequences of what we do.

THINKING: THE WIDER MORAL IMPLICATIONS

There is much debate about the 'moral dilemma'. Proposed solutions range from stricter discipline and tougher sentences for offenders to advocating a return to the 'good old days' when the ten commandments were hammered home and, supposedly, 'lived'.

All these solutions, however, are based on others 'judging' us. The 'solutions' assume acceptance of both a 'code of conduct' and 'punishment' for breaking that code. This means that fear is the 'motivator' which, admittedly, works for some in the short term but has the long-term effect of inhibiting real change and progress, because it removes the ownership of behaviour from the individual. The message, in effect, is 'Do what you want; just don't get caught'.

The world has moved on from the days when actions were determined, for example, by class structures ('I know how to act because I know my place') or threats ('If I shout loudly enough you'll do it'). This is not to say that there should not be a framework of acceptable behaviour against which individuals should judge themselves. However, that framework has to be cross-cultural and allow for individual differences. It has to be aimed at promoting individual growth rather than maintaining a status quo. The Groundrules meet these criteria.

Let's take stealing as an example. If I had been taught the Groundrules then, confronted with the opportunity to steal, I might consider my proposed actions and review them against those Groundrules in the following way:

○   **Improvement**. Will it improve my **relationship** with my girlfriend, family, friends and colleagues if I'm caught and imprisoned or if I am stigmatized as a result of my actions?
○   **Ownership**. How would I feel if someone stole something that was mine? Do I want others to feel this way?
○   **Understanding**. Have I thoroughly considered the consequences?
○   **'Can do'**. Am I looking at the complete picture? **'Can do'** may be a positive statement, but it doesn't mean 'will do' – and if I'm locked up I won't be able to do much else!

○ **Honesty**. How **honest** am I being with **myself** if I answer 'yes' to the two previous questions?

○ **Availability**. People will always know where to find me if I get caught! – but what about my **availability** to my dependants and family?

○ **Professionalism**. Perhaps my **focus** should be on positive issues – that is, how to better myself in the eyes of society as a whole – rather than on what my peers may think if I don't join them in this particular act.

By going through a conscious process in this way I may conclude that the proposed action has more disadvantages than advantages. Consequently, I may decide against it.

Thinking is about using the power of conception, judgement and inference to formulate ideas, then to view them as plausible or likely, based on either information you receive or perceive as you learn.

Thinking techniques will help you use the learning you are receiving more effectively. They allow you greater understanding of your ability to teach yourself, and to take ownership of your actions. Using thinking to understand (people, processes, information, and so on) also facilitates change, which is essential for progress and longevity.

Having explained the difference between thinking and learning, we can move on to consider how much time should be spent thinking at different levels of a company and why.

HOW MANY TIMES A WEEK SHOULD YOU DO IT?

Our brains are always working on something – sometimes on 'boring', routine tasks like making sure sufficient blood is being pumped to the heart or on the process of putting one foot in front of another. However, the 'thinking' I am referring to in this book is the process of **active consideration**.

Many, including both authors of this book, have the ability to 'think on their feet', but even so we still need to stop from time to time to reflect, analyse and conclude. It is by staring out of the window or closing your eyes and going on an internal journey, or by Mind Mapping that we discover a type of thinking that is unencumbered by any particular direction. I have, on many occasions, thought that a particular decision that someone had reached would have been quite different had they not made that decision when they were angry, busy, unhappy or under time pressure.

It is against this background that I put forward my 'unencumbered thinking time' thoughts. The percentages are not meant to be prescriptive, but directional.

THE PRINCIPAL (MANAGING DIRECTOR, CHIEF EXECUTIVE OFFICER, PRESIDENT)

The Principal's role should be centred on thinking rather than 'doing'. A Principal should aim to be 70 per cent a thinker and 30 per cent a 'doer'. Expressed another way, a Principal should be 70 per cent concerned with the future and 30 per cent looking after the present. The 'doing' part could be keeping in touch with developments in a past speciality. Alternatively, it could be carrying out agreed action points or instructing others.

Thinking, on the other hand, is looking out of the window, it's Mind Mapping®, it's anything that's generating options by thinking about them.

Talking through options clearly helps, but most talk from a Principal tends to be instructive. You have to move to a **facilitating** role, which is very much a thinking person's role. This can be very frustrating if you are used to a 'doing' role, but you must step back and allow things to happen without you. You will be surprised at the rewards that come your way.

THE SENIOR EXECUTIVE (DIRECTOR, VICE PRESIDENT, BOARD MEMBER)

Senior Executives should take on all the issues covered by the Principal's role but within their own area of responsibility. The Principal's responsibility for the company vision translates into the Senior Executive's responsibility for a departmental mission. The Senior Executive's role is to create that mission and to inspire, protect, facilitate and steer issues within their department.

The target proportions for a Senior Executive should be around 50 per cent thinking and 50 per cent doing.

THE KEY EXECUTIVE (MANAGER, TEAM LEADER)

The Key Executive, as with the Senior Executive, must cover the same areas as the Principal, but at an increasingly localized level. They must be as inspirational with their teams as Senior Executives with theirs and the Principal with the Senior Executives and the company as a whole.

At this level, the balance between thinking and doing tips a little more towards doing. I believe that Key Executives should aim to spend 60 per cent of their time doing and 40 per cent thinking. If this were achieved, both they and the company would do incredibly well.

CONCLUSION

Now you understand the nature of thinking, and how much time should be devoted to it, it's relevant to introduce some thinking techniques and discover which might work best for you.

7

DYNAMIC WAYS OF THINKING

❖

We all think with the same apparatus, the apparatus works in the same manner and we use our thinking machines similarly. However, while the processing is identical, the focus for those processes is entirely individual.

Yet, whichever focus you choose, there is a 'right' way to approach that thinking – and that is to use all your facilities. Use appropriate logic, images, speed, originality and be flexible. By 'flexible' I don't mean chaotic. Many people associate 'order' with restriction, rigidity and with feeling trapped and 'chaos' with freedom. In fact, to be structured is to be free. To be creative you need to be structured. To be free you need to be ordered, and to be ordered you need to be creative. It is a positive circle of association. You become restricted or trapped only when you are falsely, linearly, structured – that is, in a pattern which is inappropriate to the brain's functioning.

There are many thinking techniques. The five I prefer are: Mind Mapping®, force field analysis, clustering, brainstorming and Six Thinking Hats. This chapter covers each under three headings: what (the technique is designed to do), when (to use it) and how (to do it).

MIND MAPPING®

WHAT IS IT?

Mind Maps are an external representation of the way your brain works. They make use of association – encouraging the thought processes to flow naturally. The Mind Map itself then provides a written record of the output of that process, which can be easily summarized into a set of themes.

Your brain's thinking pattern is based on a gigantic, Branching Association Machine (BAM) – a super bio-computer with lines of thought radiating from a virtually infinite number of data nodes. This structure reflects the neuronal networks that make up the physical architecture of your brain.

The Mind Map is an expression of Radiant Thinking and is therefore a natural function of the human mind. It is a powerful graphic technique which provides a universal key to unlocking the potential of the brain. The Mind Map can be applied to every aspect of life where improved learning and clearer thinking will enhance human performance. It is your external expression of your own Radiant Thinking and allows you access into the vast thinking powerhouse that is your brain.

WHEN TO USE IT

Mind Mapping® can be used at any stage of the thinking process, to generate ideas individually or in groups, to summarize those ideas, and then to plan how to use them – for example, as a presentation. A Mind Map can be used to take down notes, or to plan anything from a personal shopping list through to a strategic review.

I have used Mind Mapping® for:

- creativity
- braindumping
- analysis
- problem-solving
- problem identification
- focus
- strategy
- auditing
- note-taking
- talks and presentations
- shopping lists
- prioritization
- time management
- expedition planning and review
- reasoning – for example, when buying a house or car
- book writing (this book).

Suffice it to say that I believe it is **the most complete thinking aid ever invented**.

The Mind Map® on page 98 was done by me for a court appearance in which I was attempting to reduce 6 penalty points for a speeding offence down to 3 points. I drew it whilst sitting in the waiting room of Warwick Magistrates Court.

HOW TO DO IT

Outlined below are the basic elements of Mind Mapping®. For a more detailed explanation see *The Mind Map Book: Radiant Thinking* (1993), by Tony Buzan with Barry Buzan.

1   Start in the centre of a blank piece of paper with an unframed image of the topic. Wherever possible, use colours (at least three) since they stimulate the brain.

2   Use images, symbols, codes and dimension throughout.

3   Allow your mind to wander around the subject.

4   Starting with your first thought, draw a 'branch', which is thicker at the centre where it is attached to the central image and becomes thinner as it moves away – rather like an octopus tentacle. The main branches represent your basic ordering ideas or 'chapter/subject' headings.

5   Branch thinner lines from these main branches in any direction in which your thought processes take you. Select key words and print them along each line (preferably with an image). The lines should be the same length as the word and/or image.

6   Put everything down. Don't block your thoughts and don't evaluate.

7   Don't worry about ordering or organization – once you have completed one Mind Map you can do another to plan and organize.

8   Link any associated ideas once the initial Mind Map is complete.

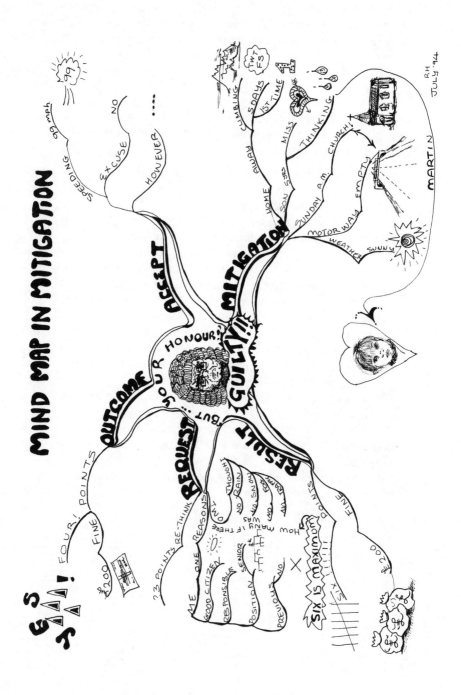

 When I decided to teach thinking techniques, the only one I insisted upon was Mind Mapping®. I also insisted that it was taught by Tony Buzan himself, the logic being that it is very rare to have an opportunity to learn about a subject from the person who has invented it because, by then, they are usually dead!

I would not be deflected! In vain did my Personnel Director talk about (lack of) budgets. In vain did Tony's team point out that he rarely built in such sessions himself and that he had a more than competent team.

Once we spoke to each other, of course, the matter was never in doubt!

Suffice it to say that his session was an overwhelmingly successful contribution to our company's development programme.

FORCE FIELD ANALYSIS

WHAT IS IT?

Force field analysis (FFA) is a framework for diagnosing a problem and then prioritizing effort in the way most likely to bring about the change needed to solve that problem. It is based on the idea that any situation, at any given time, is not static but is a dynamic equilibrium produced by two sets of interacting and opposite factors. One set of forces – the driving forces – are acting to move away from the current situation (that is, acting to bring about change) and another set – the restraining forces – are acting to maintain the status quo at best, or even to make things worse.

The principle behind FFA is therefore to identify these two sets of forces so that action can be taken to achieve the desired change. Movement can be either to strengthen or add to the driving forces or to remove and/or reduce the restraining forces. However, when considering your options, it is important to think through the implications of simply strengthening the driving forces without tackling the restraining forces since, on the basis that to every force there is an equal and opposite force, this may just have the effect of strengthening the restraining forces. Everyday illustration of this would be the more you instruct a person to change, the more determined that person becomes not to change.

WHEN TO DO IT

Use force field analysis whenever you wish to gain understanding, commitment and agreed actions in pursuit of a common goal, and also to help define what the real problem is.

HOW TO DO IT

1   **Define the problem**.
   – Describe the present state ('Where are we now?').
   – Describe the desired state ('Where do we want to be?').
2.   **Analyse the problem**.
   – List the restraining forces ('What is stopping me?').
   – List the driving forces ('What is helping me?').
   – Rank both sets of forces in order of importance.
3.   **Develop solutions**.
   – Brainstorm possible courses of action for removing and/or reducing the restraining forces.
   – Brainstorm possible courses of action for strengthening and/or adding to the driving forces.
4.   **Develop a plan**.
   – List action steps, plan resources, review.

FORCEFIELD FOR MITIGATION

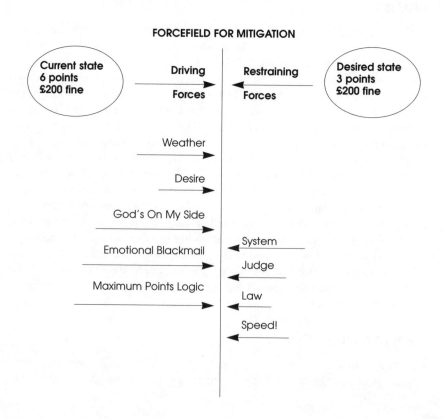

CLUSTERING

Having used any of the 'thinking techniques' designed to push you more widely in your thinking it is useful to pull back in order to be clear on the key issues and decide what you are actually going to do. This process of going wide and then focusing back in is called 'diverge and converge'.

Clustering, therefore, is a way of converging once you have diverged. It focuses your thinking before you proceed to the next stage – almost as an audit or summary of your thinking to date.

WHAT IS IT?

Clustering is sometimes known as 'content analysis'. It is the organization of large numbers of ideas into a far smaller number of categories in order to make them easier to handle or understand. The category headings or 'clusters' are derived from the original data produced so that nothing is lost.

WHEN TO USE IT

Clustering is useful as an analytical process – for example, following a creative, idea-generating session. Typically it might be used:

○　　after a brainstorming session
○　　to structure findings from interviews or questionnaires
○　　to grouping restraining or driving forces when completing a force field analysis.

HOW TO USE IT

The clusters are found through a process of trial and error which can take some time. Clustering can be done in groups or individually.

1　　Read all the data generated. As you do so, jot down themes, headings or common ideas that seem to emerge. The aim is to produce a set of independent headings with no overlaps between them.

2　　Check the headings by sorting all the ideas under the headings you have produced. A quick way to do this is to write all the ideas on Post-it Notes and then arrange them under the headings. Once this has been done ask someone else to categorize a sample of the ideas. They should put the sample ideas under the same headings or clusters as you have.

3　　Group all the remaining ideas under the appropriate cluster headings.

CLUSTERING FOR MITIGATION

Driving Forces

1 Weather
2 Desire
3 God's On My Side
4 Emotional Blackmail
5 Maximum Points Logic

Restraining Forces

System   1
Judge   1
Law   2
Speed   2

BRAINSTORMING

Brainstorming can be very creative, but there are three key rules:

1   Run a warm-up session on a far-fetched topic.
2   Write down all that you think – don't question.
3   Do it quickly, or set a time limit.

Once you have carried out FFA (gone wide) and then clustered (homed in), it is useful to take the clustered issues and brainstorm them on the original problem.

WHAT IS IT?

Brainstorming is a means of generating a large number of ideas in a very short space of time. This technique is often used by groups of people, but it is also possible to brainstorm on an individual basis. For me, brainstorming works better on an individual basis, and research explains why. When you have someone writing on a board and many people shouting out their thoughts, you begin a process of gravitational pull towards a particular idea or person. For example, if you were looking for ideas on how to increase profits and someone shouts out 'sell some assets', there will be a natural pull towards the idea of selling and subsequent ideas will reflect this. If, however, you are on your own this doesn't happen. Researchers also found that the individual was likely to generate a greater number of different ideas than a group. It is therefore beneficial to use a combination of individual and group brainstorming sessions.

WHEN TO USE IT

Use brainstorming at the point when creativity is needed either to devise a way around a specific problem or in a wider context – for example, to generate ideas for new products.

HOW TO USE IT

There are some guidelines which those involved must understand:

1   **Suspend judgement** – in order not to evaluate ideas before they have been fully expressed and to prevent barriers (for example, 'that's stupid') hindering the process.
2   **Freewheel** – in order to make use of association.
3   **Generate quantity** – in order to produce as many ideas as possible. At this point, quality is not the aim.
4   **Cross-fertilize** – using an idea from someone else to spark another.

Traditionally, brainstorming has been carried out by listing the words or ideas you have thought of but a much more modern and efficient method is described in Chapter 6 of Tony Buzan's *The Mind Map Book*. Here, Tony takes the brainstorming concept and demonstrates how the process can:

○   generate more than ten times the standard number of brainstormed ideas by:
    –   using images to improve the quality of innovation
    –   using colour to literally make the brainstorming session more 'colourful'
○   reflect, as a result, the fundamentally infinite nature of the brain and its idea-generating capacity, rather than the truncated thinking that the listing approach provides.

Before you tackle your real issue it is, as I've said, a good idea to put your brain into gear with a simple 'warm-up session'. Choose something unrelated to your real topic in order to start your brain freewheeling. An example is given below.

WARM-UP EXAMPLE: WHAT CAN BE DONE WITH A SHOE?

The ideas illustrated above were written in 60 seconds. Their degree of usefulness is irrelevant at this stage. The point is that I have begun the process of thinking more creatively.

Having warmed up I can now tackle the main menu.

The next steps are:

1   to carry on until I exhaust my ideas
2   to leave for a while, then go back to review and refresh
3   to ask my colleagues to do the same and compare
4   to compile a master brainstorming Mind Map.

Returning to an earlier point, I would suggest that, after the warm-up session, it is useful to begin with individual brainstorming, then move to group brainstorming, then back to individual and finish with a group session to get maximum benefit from the technique.

SIX THINKING HATS

WHAT IS IT?

Six Thinking Hats is a technique devised by Edward de Bono. A more detailed explanation of the thinking behind it and the technique can be obtained from his book *Six Thinking Hats* (1990). In summary, however, it is a way of unscrambling the different types of thinking that take place in the brain.

When using this technique, rather than try to use all the thinking hats at once, as in conventional discussion and argument, each type of thinking is identified and recognized as having equal weight but as bringing a different angle to any given topic (something like members of a team).

Although this conscious 'unscrambling' may seem an artificial way of conducting a discussion it is this very artificiality that gives it more structure and focus. The concept of the hat allows individuals to express thoughts that otherwise may either be unarticulated or perceived as 'unacceptable' or 'soft'.

The six hats, in the order in which they could be used to guide a meeting, are as follows:

- ○ **White (clouds)**: for pure facts, figures and information
- ○ **Red (fire)**: for feelings, emotions, hunches and intuition
- ○ **Black (storm)**: for the Devil's Advocate, negative judgement, 'why it won't work'
- ○ **Yellow (sun)**: for brightness, optimism, positive and constructive ideas, 'why it will work'
- ○ **Green (field)**: for creative, provocative, lateral thoughts
- ○ **Blue (sky)**: for thinking about the overview, summarizing for action

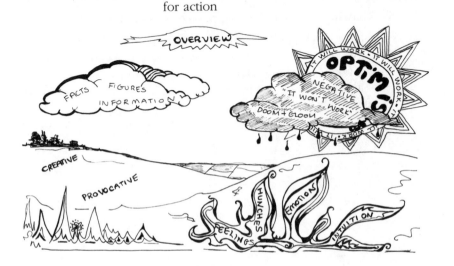

To remember the hats, I tend to relate them to the environment. So **blue** is the sky (overview), **white** is cloud (snow-white, pure), **yellow** is the sun (bright, cheerful), **green** is fields (vast, produces wonders), **black** is a storm (doom and gloom) and **red** is fire (emotion).

WHEN TO USE IT

Six Thinking Hats can be used whenever a group is becoming jaded in order to create new ideas. It is also useful, particularly with senior teams, for encouraging the expression of emotional issues, surrounding the topic under discussion, which might otherwise have been suppressed. In addition, it is a good 'auditing' tool once a course of action has been decided on.

As a Principal you can also use it to prevent your team becoming too 'cosy'. If, for example, you feel that a project is merely being 'nodded through', ask for a 'black hat session', so that everyone has to consider or 'imagine' some negative aspects. If the project is still passed, you will feel reassured that its potential disadvantages and problems have been explored but without unproductive and personal conflict.

HOW TO USE IT

The procedure described below applies to a group problem-solving session. However, it is also easy to use Six Thinking Hats within a normal conversation – for example, 'OK, we've agreed on that course of action. Let's just "Red Hat" [or "Black Hat"] it, for a minute'.

As with all thinking techniques, you can also use Six Thinking Hats on your own as well as with a group.

The Six Thinking Hats structured approach is as follows:

1   The meeting should be led but not directed.
2   The topic is agreed in terms that everyone understands.
3   Using traditional brainstorming rules, the group brainstorms the problem six times, each time 'wearing' a different hat in the sequence given in page 105.
4   Ideas are recorded, using a clean sheet of paper for each of the separate six sessions.

A CASE STUDY OF COMBINED THINKING TECHNIQUES

As I have said, these thinking techniques can be used singly, but I have found that it is much more useful and powerful to combine them. In this real-life case study I outline the process I used for making important decisions at Burmah Petroleum Fuels Ltd. The key in combining thinking techniques is to know what each is designed to achieve and to use it at the relevant point. The aim is to use the techniques as a tool, not to get them technically perfect every time! When I described the teaching of these techniques as 'dynamic', I meant it in two senses: first, using these techniques 'fires people up', and gets things moving, second, the techniques themselves can be used in a dynamic way – you can add to them, combine them and evolve them.

BACKGROUND

When I first joined Burmah Petroleum Fuels Ltd my brief was simple. Burmah Castrol (the parent company) realized that what they had in BPFL was not what they wanted. Although they knew that the company was not pursuing any clearly defined strategy, they nevertheless had no 'feel' for what this strategy ought to be. In particular, they did not feel sufficiently confident to implement any direction based on their own knowledge of the forecourt industry, which was where BPFL traded. I think it showed great strength to recognize and act on this perception and I will always be grateful to them for doing so.

FINDING THE WAY FORWARD

I knew the industry well. I also knew that BPFL had a poor image. The first task therefore had to be data-gathering. I set about pulling together information from every conceivable source, internally, and also embarked on a ten-week project with external consultants to obtain information on the industry, an assessment of where BPFL fitted into it and, based on a series of options, a view of what type of company BPFL could be.

Once I had this mass of information I wanted to 'see the whole picture'. I therefore used Mind Mapping™ as a starting point. I have been a compulsive Mind Mapper for some 15 years and nowadays I even think in Mind Map form, in the sense that I can visualize my central theme and create branch (main issue) themes, and then twigs (detail).

Figure 7.1 is an edited (to protect the innocent) version of my initial Mind Map for BPFL. The first thing you'll notice is the central image. This is my version of Burmah Castrol's mystical Chinthe, two of which were

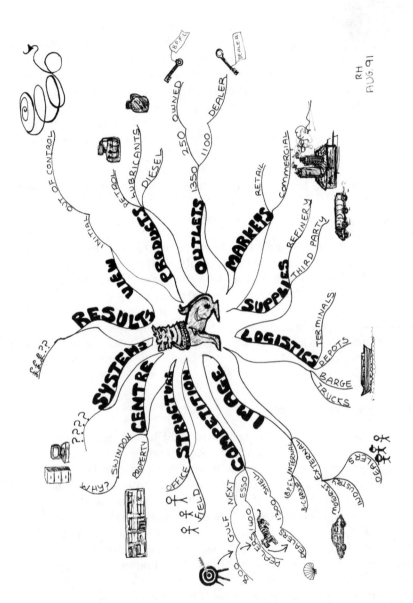

Figure 7.1   Initial Mind Map for BPFL

brought from Burma, blessed by Buddhist priests, and have been standing outside the Burmah Castrol headquarters since it opened in 1973. I chose this image because it says so much and is more memorable than a word. Other key points to note are:

○   In just 40 words, I have summarized the main points of some 12–14 weeks' work.

○   You will be able to look at this Mind Map and understand much of it. When I began to re-create it for this book, all the issues, in the most minute detail, flooded back. For me, one of the key advantages of Mind Mapping® is that it aids memory.

Some of the reports and research behind these keywords began to paint a picture of a complex company, but it was a company that had merely evolved, rather than been planned. Management controls were weak, staff understanding was poor and effective communication almost non-existent. Overall, my Mind Map gave me a picture of a company out of control.

To examine the problem more analytically I used force field analysis.

My answer to the question 'Where am I?' was 'Out of control'. I knew, in my heart, that 'where I wanted to be' was to see BPFL at No. 1 in its field, and also, culturally, everything that I have always believed in (now called the Thinking Organization).

At this stage the most obvious move would have been to try to go from 'out of control' to 'No. 1/Thinking Organization'. This, I believed, would, however, have failed because it was too big a leap, although it is important to note that it remained my long-term aim. What I realized when considering my response to the original 'Where do I want to be?' question was that any accidental success we achieved would be wasted without a means of controlling and sustaining that success.

In my mind I took a small step but, in reality, still gave myself a huge task. I re-created my force field in a 'moment in time' and it looked like this:

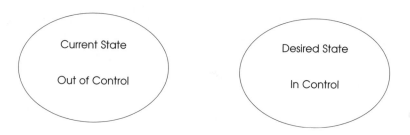

Current State

Out of Control

Desired State

In Control

This was a difficult step for me, because I am no control freak. Yet, in hindsight it was the step that facilitated ultimate success.

Having decided where I was and where I wanted to be, I could add the 'driving' and 'restraining' forces which looked something like this:

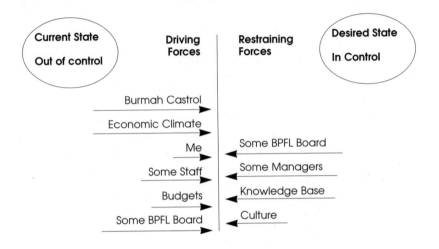

For me force field analysis had highlighted a number of issues. There were many more, and I needed to be able to focus in order to prioritize for action. I followed up with the clustering technique and, for BPFL my clusters were, broadly, like this:

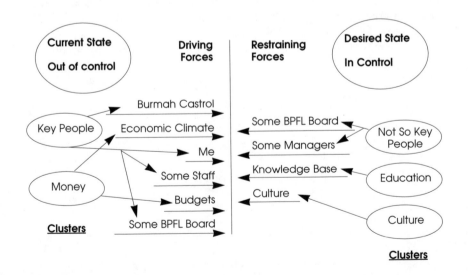

This process made the key issues very obvious. To find a way forward and consider my options I decided to brainstorm my clusters. However, I felt that I did not need to brainstorm on 'key people' or 'money' in the 'drivers' clusters, nor on 'not so key people' or 'education' in the 'restrainers'. What leapt out was 'culture'. This was the problem – and, anyway, it encompassed all the other issues. It was **the** input, since, if I changed the culture the other components would automatically fall into place, as outcomes.

Fundamentally, I had to decide how to change from a loose method of operation to a controlled one. Simply instructing the employees might work. On the other hand, creating an environment in which change was natural would be certain to yield the outcome I wanted. My difficulty was time pressure – I needed to progress onward and upward rapidly.

I was unable to formulate anything coherent on paper about this, so I decided to separate the words 'change' and 'culture' and brainstorm them, yielding something like the following results:

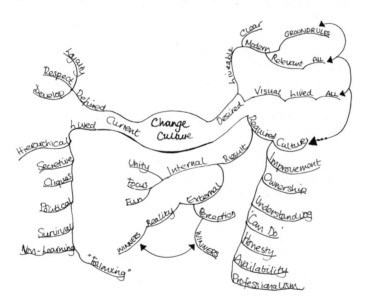

Once again I applied clustering to the process to obtain some focus. The fundamental points emerging from this were as follows:

○   The key to the desired outcome was people, not processes.
○   Teaching was as important as telling.

Later, I came to regard teaching as key as I discovered that teaching people to learn from experience – good and bad – and demonstrating how doing something differently would work gave results that would be more likely to last.

Having Mind Mapped, carried out a force field analysis, clustered, brainstormed and clustered again to devise what I considered to be the way forward, I decided to check how I felt about my current position. To do this I used Six Hat Thinking. Here's the result of applying the technique to my decision to '**concentrate on people not processes**'.

○ **White hat (facts):**
   – There are 600 directly employed people (many different types of location).
   – A further 4000 (minimum) will be indirectly influenced on sites.
   – There's no training facility.
   – There will be objections.
   – Speed is important.
   – There's no Personnel Director.

○ **Red hat (feelings):**
   – It may be too slow.
   – I'm on my own (the Board isn't behind me).
   – Most staff will welcome it.

○ **Black hat (Devil's Advocate):**
   – The Board will interfere and stop it working.
   – The staff are not capable.
   – Burmah Castrol Group won't like it.
   – I may have to replace people – this will cost money.

○ **Yellow hat (optimism):**
   – I've done it, so anyone can.
   – The staff will want to learn.
   – It will create a great company.
   – It will produce long-term rewards.
   – It will be recognized, externally, that we've changed.
   – It will be a tremendous achievement.
   – The costs of replacing staff will be outweighed by the benefits.

○ **Green hat (creative):**
   – I could lead the programme.
   – I could create my own programme.
   – I could find positive staff and ask them to teach.
   – I will open a training centre.
   – I will offer this to customers as well as staff.
   – I could create a '100 Club' for the 100+%ers.
   – I could give awards for success.

○ **Blue hat (overview):**
   – I need to sort out the structure first.

- I need to identify unsupportive staff.
- I must prepare a proposal for the Board.
- I must communicate with staff.
- I must communicate with Burmah Castrol.
- I must talk to consultants on design.
- I need to open a training centre.
- I need to discuss a '100 Club'.

Having gone through this process, I could clearly see another Mind Map attack coming on. I produced the one depicted in Figure 7.2 as my final, detailed, action plan.

Mind Map attacks

Although I have, so far, described the use of Mind Maps in logical processes, it is also true that I have panic attacks for which the only known cure is a Mind Map! Examples would be:

O   being in court on a speeding offence and realizing, after a conversation with the prosecution, that I had not thought through my arguments (see page 98)

O   being asked at very short notice to give a speech

O   needing to give feedback on a complex subject in a meeting where many people have given their views.

As someone who has always managed to keep several balls in the air at the same time, now and then I feel the need to Mind Map how they are going to come down, where they are going to come down, in what order and whether I will be underneath any of them!

I have tried many remedies for a hangover and have not been able to cure the condition. However, Mind Maps have solved 100 per cent of my panic attacks by helping me see the bigger picture.

The process I've described over the last few pages is illustrated by the diagram on page 115. One of the keys to building the kind of company I needed was to teach these techniques and others to employees. This was a tremendously exciting and rewarding process – for the company, for those involved and for me. In the following section I outline a few notes on what works particularly well for me when teaching others.

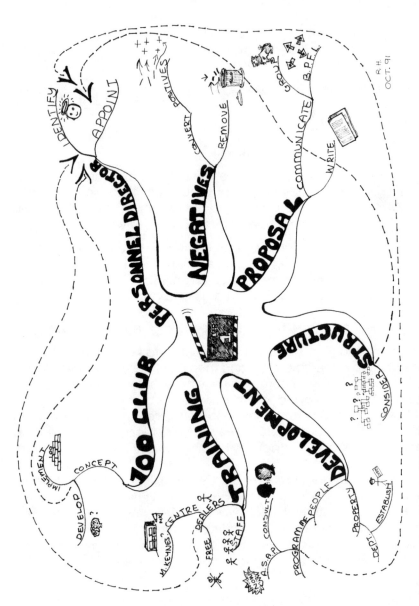

Figure 7.2   The final, detailed BPFL action plan

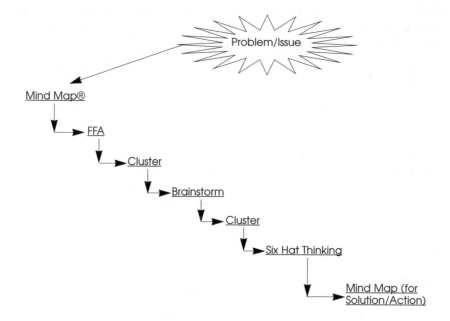

TEACHING TECHNIQUES

GROUP/SOLO

When teaching thinking techniques, you can multiply the effect of groupwork many times by asking the group to use a single or combination of techniques, individually, to solve a problem, then come together, discuss and create group solutions. The results can be quite staggering.

 We had some great fun in the group sessions we ran in BPFL. To understand, you need to know that if I ever (and I did!) become annoyed with someone, there was a stock statement which I apparently used, and which I was unaware of until this incident. This statement was 'My Mum could have done that (that is, made the same mistake as you) and she would have cost me less than you!'

In one session we were teaching scenario planning (basically anticipating potential situations and planning what to do if they occurred) to drive home the learning point that you don't wait for a disaster to happen to think through your planning.

The scenario given was a newspaper headline which they had read over breakfast: 'Rikki Hunt and Entire BPFL Board Quit to Join

Shell – Shock'. After about 30 minutes of debate, the group called back our consultant, David Simmons, and myself and proudly presented their plan of action: 'Recruit Rikki's Mum!'.

CASE STUDIES

Only use real-life case studies or problems that people can relate to. This way, people see instantly how to use the techniques in their daily work – and do.

For example, asking a group of information technology specialists to apply the thinking techniques to 'improving manufacturing output' will not work. Although the techniques may be of some help to them in tackling the problem, it is daunting and unnecessary to give them a subject outside their speciality when you are introducing something new.

TIMING

You may be excused for thinking that you would not have time to use any, let alone a combination, of the thinking techniques, given that your problem or opportunity is with you now, not some time in the future.

You would be wrong. With practice you could do the complete combination on BPFL described earlier in just 45 minutes. For example, Mind Maps can be completed in five to ten minutes.

It is important to emphasize this point when teaching, and also to show how much faster people become with practice in order to encourage them to persevere.

 In BPFL the teaching of thinking techniques had a massive effect. Clearly, this was, in part, due to the techniques themselves, but there was more to it than that....

In beginning a programme with the Groundrules as its foundation and which, amongst other things, created the environment for continuous learning and change, I also gave people a massive opportunity to use their brains in a way never before considered. They grabbed this opportunity very firmly with both hands and, today, talking to those involved, it is no surprise to find that they:

O   continue to use the Groundrules as a foundation for re-creating the thinking environment in their new companies (including those setting up their own companies)
O   continue to use thinking techniques (predominantly Mind Mapping®)
O   continue to progress.

The fact that they do this when they don't have to also shows that they clearly see the benefits for themselves and consequently choose to think and act in these ways. It proves that the Thinking Organization is not a 'quick-fix fad' but a way of life.

APPENDIX: OTHER THINKING TECHNIQUES

There are many and varied thinking techniques available to you. More are briefly described below.

ATTRIBUTE LISTING

The main attributes of the idea, object and/or problem are listed and examined in turn to see how they might be changed.

BACKWARD FISHBONE

Instead of looking at all the possible causes of a problem or effect, this technique investigates the effects or possible problems associated with a proposed course of action – in other words, tests it. (**De Bono's Six Thinking Hats does this**.)

BASIC FISHBONE

This is used by a group to work through a known problem to identify likely causes and how they interact with each other.

CHECKLISTS

Checklists can be used to stimulate new ideas or prevent ideas being left out. The technique includes Osborn's list of questions which include: 'Put to other uses?', 'Modify?', 'Reverse?', 'Combine?' and so on.

COGNITIVE MAPPING

This method involves creating a diagram of all the parts and/or issues of a given topic or problem, describing (qualitatively and quantitatively) and indicating their influence on each other. (**Mind Mapping® does this better**.)

CONCEPT FAN

This technique involves taking an issue, establishing key directions in which that issue could go, examining the concepts involved in each of those directions and, finally, devising ideas/suggestions that relate to each concept.

CRITERIA TESTING

This technique is also known as weighting. It evaluates and compares alternative solutions by rating them against a set of weighted criteria. (**Mind Mapping® is a useful tool for creating the alternative solutions in the first place**.)

FILTERING

This technique eliminates the least useful ideas, by agreeing a set of 'hurdles', – based on objective criteria – that each idea needs to overcome in order to move to the next stage.

FLOWCHARTS

Flowcharts are a visual method of presenting information on plans or processes. They are useful for data collection, investigation and project planning. (**Mind Mapping® does these better**.)

FORCED RELATIONSHIPS

This is a creative technique in which two or more objects or ideas are taken and the question is asked 'How many ways can these be combined to make a new idea/object?'.

IDEA WRITING

This is a similar technique to brainstorming, in which groups generate/develop ideas from each other's ideas instead of just coming up with different ones.

LIST MAKING

This, quite simply, is what it says. The aim is to compile as many ideas as possible, without evaluation, in a short space of time. (**Mind Mapping® is also very useful for this**.)

MORPHOLOGICAL FORCED CONNECTIONS

This technique looks at all the variables in a matrix and attempts to combine them in new ways.

PARETO 80–20 RULE

This is a mechanism for identifying which problems, if solved, will have the greatest effect. Based on the 80–20 rule – that is, 80 per cent of wealth is owned by 20 per cent of the people; 80 per cent of problems is caused by 20 per cent of employees and so on. The Pareto diagram analyses issues to allow prioritization of action. (**It would be useful to apply this to clustered points from a force field analysis**.)

RANDOM STARTERS

Makes use of everyday objects as a source of inspiration. For example, you choose an object at random and consider ways of relating it to a problem.

REVERSE BRAINSTORMING (DEVIL'S ADVOCATE)

This technique is used after evaluation. It is based on asking the question 'How likely is this idea to fail?'. (**De Bono's 'black hat' does this, and is more fun**.)

RICH PICTURES

This technique entails making a visual summary of the problem or issue under discussion while gathering information on it. The pictures produced lead to other issues and/or decisions on other information needed. (**Mind Mapping® is better**.)

SCENARIO PLANNING

This technique investigates the 'What ifs?' but aims beyond merely extrapolating what exists now.

STRUCTURED INTERVIEWS

This is a common framework for a series of interviews, aiming to get information, try out ideas, generate new ideas and so on.

SWOT ANALYSIS

SWOT analysis identifies the strengths, weaknesses, opportunities and threats in any given area for the purposes of discussion and/or action planning (**It is useful to follow a SWOT analysis with clustering. The clustered points can then become the main branches of a Mind Map**.)

WHY–HOW? CHARTING

This aims to promote a combination of abstract and concrete thinking by asking a series of 'why' questions about a particular issue and then proceeding to ask 'how' questions. (**De Bono's Six Thinking Hats does this most effectively**.)

WILDEST IDEA

This is a creative technique in which the wildest/most outrageous idea from a brainstorming session is taken with the aim of turning it into a 'good', possibly workable, idea.

SUMMARY

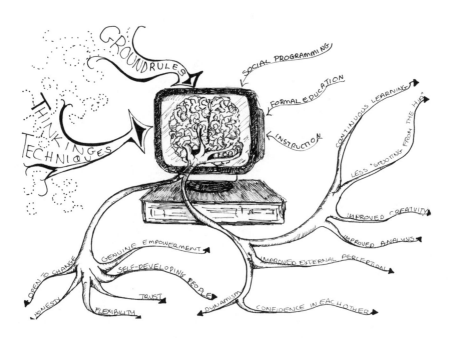

Having seen the benefits of adding the Groundrules software to our basic model, we have now added the thinking techniques. The result is a person who has a great attitude and the tools (thinking techniques) to be a winner.

THE THINKING ORGANIZATION

The Thinking Organization:

- ○ **has a physically and mentally fit workforce**
- ○ **teaches thinking and improves the quality of learning**
- ○ **helps all to value and use all types of thinking**
- ○ **gives people tools to solve problems**
- ○ **creates leaders who actively spend time 'thinking'.**

ACTION PLAN

1   Having discovered some facts about the brain that you probably didn't know, get excited and start to put your brain into gear!

2   Analyse how much time you spend thinking (not doing, worrying or fire-fighting) and plan how to increase it. Gradually you will see results.

3   Try some of the techniques – on simple issues at first.

4   Don't be put off if you don't have 'brain flashes' straightaway. They do come; just persevere. Try mind sports – chess, 'Go', memory games, more crosswords from different sources. Make up your own.

5   Play mind sports with your children or someone else's. Ask them to tell you stories and, above all, lobby your local school or education authority to begin the process of true learning by teaching 'thinking'.

REVIEW BY TONY BUZAN

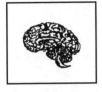 It is useful, at this juncture, to revisit the deeper meanings behind the word 'thinking'. When we consider such words as 'deliberate', 'meditate', 'reason', 'reflect', 'speculate' 'contemplate', 'ponder', 'envision', 'imagine', 'visualize' and 'conceive' we have tended to think of them in the traditional thinking styles (that is, as academic functions dominated by logic, analysis, words and numbers). A true Thinking Organization must perceive these thinking areas in a much broader light.

Here, it is useful to review the research into the left and right cortical hemispheres initiated by Roger Sperry in the 1960s. This confirmed that each of the two hemispheres is dominant in a different set of thinking skills. The left hemisphere tends to be dominant in logic, lists, lines, words, number and analysis – the so-called, business, academic or intellectual skills – whereas the right hemisphere is dominant in rhythm, colour, daydreaming, imagination, spatial awareness and gestalt (seeing the whole patterns) – the so-called creative, artistic, emotional and intuitive skills.

If you put this brain research into the context of our traditional mode of 'thinking about thinking', with the emphasis placed on 'left-brain' skills throughout our education system, you will see that we have literally trained ourselves to be 'half-wits'! Indeed, we have been trained to use only 50 per cent of the intellectual thinking skills allotted to us.

Ironically this 50 per cent may possibly plummet to below 1 per cent if we take into account the fact that the multiple fingers of intelligence represented by skills of the two hemispheres act synergetically. If you use 50 per cent of your legs to run, your efficiency is considerably diminished!

In view of the above, **all** the comments in Part II should be considered in the light of the much vaster range of skills that the Thinking Organization has at its fingertips (or its dendritic tips!).

Imagine an organization in which all the employees/owners applied all the appropriate dynamic thinking techniques whilst simultaneously using a much greater vocabulary, an accelerated and much greater facility with numbers, an enhanced ability to analyse and think logically, a much more vast imagination and an ability to use that imagination, and a more musical, rhythmic and colourful approach to both business and life. Then add to all this an ability to see, with vivid clarity, the detail and simultaneous capacity to grasp and conquer the larger and complex pictures, maps and visions of the future. **That is the beauty and potential of the Thinking Organization**.

Unlocking this massive potential, however, has to be a conscious set of actions unleashed by those who lead those organizations.

It is becoming increasingly apparent that the individuals and organizations that will lead business in the future are those who and which develop themselves on all levels and who can become leaders not by chance or by hope, but by a dedicated focus on their vision, their mission and the mutual development of thinking skills in those who work with them. Such skills will not, however, fulfil their ultimate potential unless they are given the opportunity to flourish in the right environment – the Thinking Organization environment created through applying the Groundrules.

In the new 'brain-led', not 'brain-dead', organization, leadership itself is 'whole-brain'. It has to be 'meta leadership'. The characteristics, skills and thinking needed to achieve such meta leadership is explored in Part III.

PART III
LEADING IN THE ENVIRONMENT

❖

INTRODUCTION TO PART III

 *'"Meta" leaders understand why others follow them and are comfortable to follow when needed.' (Rikki Hunt)*

You have now read about the absolute necessity of creating the environment for a Thinking Organization, understood the importance of thinking in that environment and had an introduction to some thinking techniques. Part III discusses the critical requirement for leadership in that environment.

Just because you have a desire to create a Thinking Organization does not mean that you will be able to do so. Using the thinking techniques does not mean that a Thinking Organization will automatically follow – although it is fair to say that if, at this stage of the book, you are raring to go and have accepted all the ideas you will stand a better chance of creating your Thinking Organization than the person who has not.

Part III is the final piece of the jigsaw. To achieve everything outlined so far you will have to be not just 'a leader', not just a 'great leader' but a 'meta leader' – going beyond what is currently expected and using all your skills continuously. This Part gives you some ideas on how to go about this.

Chapter 8 questions the nature of leadership. This is a vital area, particularly in terms of moving away from conventional programming which suggests that great leadership is the domain of a few, exceptional, people. Certainly, there are fewer leaders than followers and, whilst it is true that not everyone wants to lead, there are many who could make excellent leaders if only they would discard their existing thinking (that word again!) and preconceptions of their own ability.

Were we to understand that anyone **can** lead, we would take more responsibility for our ultimate destination. **Our situation today is the result of our leadership of ourselves yesterday**. Understanding this allows much greater ownership of our actions.

In this chapter leadership is discussed under a number of headings, the first of which is the origin of leadership – is it a characteristic we are born with or has it been learned? The chapter then moves on to look at the characteristics of effective leaders, considering first of all what gives each leader power. This is achieved through the application of a new concept called the 'Powerbase of Leadership' – a tool which provides a means of analysing such power and shows how, if there are gaps, it is possible to fill them. It then identifies other characteristics shown by effective leaders and the different styles of leadership. This is followed by the introduction of a way to help you 'let go' of one type of job as you move up to another by means of a model called the 'Circle of Knowledge' which helps analyse where the specialist knowledge base in a company is and where it should be. We've all met entrepreneurs who know everything about their company and find it difficult to let go, even though they must in order for the company to progress. This model has been used successfully to point out to leaders within organizations how, by their insistence in being the specialist in everything, they hold their people, and ultimately their company, back and, as a result, have a workforce that will never be truly empowered.

The chapter concludes with a look at one of the ways in which a leader can help others develop – through mentoring.

Chapter 9 'Perception Rules' is based on the idea that it is not what we think we are that is important in the world. It isn't even what we actually are. It is what others **think we are** that is important. Since understanding how we are perceived by our followers, amongst others, will help us understand ourselves as leaders, it is useful to check others' views of ourselves. This chapter describes the Saville & Holdsworth PRS method of doing this.

'Change' is one of the most discussed words in business today, and yet many do not have a good working definition for the process. Chapter 10 covers this subject comprehensively, including types of change, barriers to change, why some people just won't change (and what to do about it) and, finally, the role of the leader in change.

Part III concludes with a summary, an action plan and a review by Tony Buzan.

8
META LEADERSHIP

DEFINING A LEADER

Here are just some of the ways in which different people have defined a leader:

> Reason and calm judgement, the qualities especially belonging to a leader. (Tacitus)

> Leaders must be seen to be up front, up to date, up to their job and up early in the morning. (Lord Sieff)

> ... the art of inspiring others to give of their best and the courage to use this art. (Lord Hunt)

> 'I lead by example and persuasion and a hell of a lot of hard work ... one has to create the conditions in which people want to give of their best.' (Sir John Harvey-Jones)

My own definition is:
'"Meta" leaders understand why others follow them and are comfortable to follow when needed.' (Rikki Hunt)

Unless we truly understand our followers' individual needs, desires, motivations, perceived limits, abilities and so on we will not be able to get the best from them. Understanding why people follow at a certain point in time is essential.

THE NEED FOR LEADERSHIP

Imagine a world where there are no leaders and you will envisage chaos and disorder. Without someone, be they elected or self-selected, leading the way, it is difficult to see how we would get anything done. It's bad enough with leaders who create red tape, which is just another way of saying 'Here's why you can't do it!'. In reality – rather like the orchestra without a conductor, which may keep going for some minutes after the conductor has left but which will eventually cascade into a cacophony of chaos – at some point we all need to be given a direction in which to travel.

Even in today's environment of outsourcing and down- or 'right'-sizing, someone somewhere has to make a decision which will affect others. The current wisdom is that tomorrow's organizations will be non-hierarchical, team-based and project-led. Even if this were true, and I'm not sure that it is, all teams still need a team leader. Even if the role is seen as team coordinator, someone has to summarize the views of the team and be prepared to make decisions.

The difference between managing and leading is not as complex as some would have us believe.

You manage processes. You lead people.

BORN LEADER?

We are learning a great deal, today, about the brain – information which, only 20 years ago, we could only guess at.

Traditionally psychologists have made much of the concept of the 'gang' or 'playground' leader, predicting that a child demonstrating leadership qualities at a very early age would become the industrial leader of tomorrow. Equally, those who 'followed' in the playground were destined to be the 'worker ant' of the future. A more logical view is that we all develop at different rates. Whilst some 'playground leaders' undoubtedly sustain those skills through to adulthood, some seem to lose them and other 'worker ants' develop them later in life. This 'worker ant', like any other, **can** become a leader.

I was very clearly a worker ant until, at the tender age of 15, it was suggested to me that it would be better if I left school. I dutifully took the advice given to me and found that, from that day on, my education began. This is covered in the short account of my 'journey' that appears in 'Introducing the Authors' but, for those who skipped it, this included being sent by my employer and his right-hand man on his market stall business for 'buckets of steam', 'skyhooks' and 'long waits' in Dewhurst's the butchers in St Chad's Parade, Kirkby, Liverpool – as well as being sent to the aforementioned butchers to have a meat cleaver repointed (four times)!

The point is that what I am today is the result of a very complex cocktail. This includes influences from my family – particularly in the area of values or ethics – friends, education and experiences plus the formation of my own opinions, using all of the above. I believe I evolved into a leader; I was not born as one.

What follows is a tool I developed to help identify some key cornerstones of leadership. Identifying these four cornerstones makes it a simple task to imagine how you are perceived as a leader, particularly if, like most people, you lack one or more of them. It then becomes equally clear what has to be done to help you develop the missing pieces of that leadership jigsaw.

THE POWERBASE OF LEADERSHIP

Any leader has one or more of the following as a powerbase:

Powerbases	Definition
Position:	Has a job with one or more people reporting to it.
Knowledge:	Specialist or technical knowledge (here, 'management' is seen as a specialist subject).
Communication:	The ability to have the message you want to give received. Takes into account the need to listen and to be able to translate the message in a way which is appropriate to different audiences.
Charisma:	'Presence', a personality that cannot be ignored; an ability to draw others together.

The ideal is, of course, to have all four 'bases'. This type of leader has:

○   the **position** to achieve action
○   sufficient **knowledge** of the subject to know what needs doing
○   the ability to **communicate** clearly what is needed
○   **charisma** – the magnetism to pull people together for a common cause.

However, given that few are this perfect, it is worth considering the impact of various combinations of these elements.

To give an idea of what this might mean, a few thoughts on the implications of one or more powerbases being missing are outlined below. This is followed by a method of handling that situation. It is most important to realize that, just because there are gaps, a person is not doomed to everlasting imperfection! In fact, by using the Groundrules and thinking techniques, all of the potential gaps can be plugged.

MISSING ELEMENTS

WITH charisma, communication, knowledge; WITHOUT position

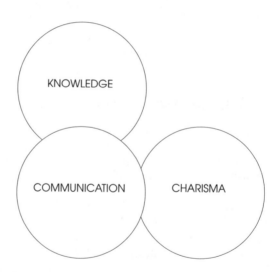

This combination can be dangerous. An organization which is unable to provide the position that is needed, or which is seen as deserved, risks, in the long term, that person using the power they do have (that is, knowledge, communication skills and charisma) in negative ways.

Someone in this situation may use their knowledge base to good effect, convincing those below, or even at the same level, that they know better than those in positions of power. You can imagine that, when you take into account their good communication skills and charisma, you have a potentially powerful cocktail for unrest.

WITH position, communication knowledge; WITHOUT charisma

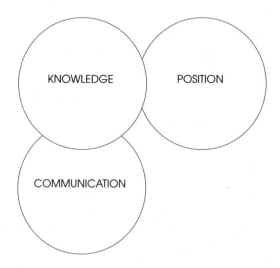

Here is a person with knowledge of the subject, issue or company, who is good at communicating what they want to achieve and in a position to do something about it. However, their lack of charisma means that they are not perceived as dynamic, or passionate.

What can happen with this type of leader is that the best plan, put forward using total knowledge and communicated clearly from a position of strength, does not inspire the level of commitment it deserves because the followers are not excited by it – they are not 'hooked' into it.

WITH position, charisma, knowledge; WITHOUT communication

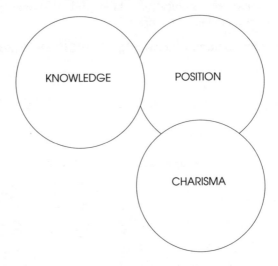

This is an immensely frustrating combination. Here is someone technically qualified, passionate about what they want to achieve, in a position to do so but unable to 'translate' that into language which followers can understand. This can lead to lack of focus and fragmented implementation because of differing interpretations of what is wanted.

WITH position, charisma, communication; WITHOUT knowledge

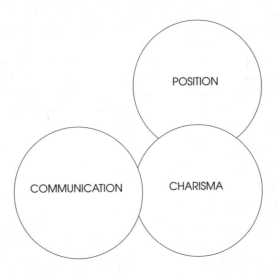

This is an extremely interesting combination. Here we have someone with a position from which they can act, communication skills to translate desired actions to others effectively and charisma to create excitement and hunger for winning in their followers. **But** they lack knowledge about the subject or issue. The result can be catastrophic. You are being led from the front by a strongly charismatic communicator, **but** you are being led in the wrong direction.

FILLING POWERBASE GAPS

The good news is that any of the gaps described above can be filled by following the steps outlined below.

Step 1: Agree the gap

Get the person involved to realize and agree that a gap exists. In Chapter 9 I discuss personality profiling, which is a helpful tool. I find that the gap that exists is often visible to many other people (manager, peers, subordinates) but not to the person concerned. Completing a personality questionnaire is a visual way of showing that others perceive a gap to be present.

Step 2: Discuss the gap and its impact

Point out that most people have gaps of one sort or another and that recognizing its existence is halfway to filling it. You have a problem only if you are unaware of it.

Discuss the impact of the gap on all the relationships in which that person is involved. Give examples of problems which are caused as a result of the gap.

Apply the 'perfect' person (that is, with no gaps) to the Groundrules Review process. Point out how the 'perfect' leader lives the Groundrules more fully. Then apply the Groundrules to the person concerned and highlight the obvious shortcomings. For example, someone who displays the negative behaviour shown under 'without position' will not score highly on:

○ **Improvement: Relationships**, in particular, will not be improved by someone who is continuously criticizing others.

○ **Ownership**: Again, bad-mouthing, and continually maintaining that 'it won't work' is not owning the **direction**. This type of person is also likely to be sarcastic about **successes** – attributing them to luck rather than effort.

○ **Understanding**: Such a person is unlikely to be **listening**, nor will they **accept** others' objectives and motivations.

○ **'Can do'**: They probably take a **negative** stance on most issues

○ and may not **help others** except where there is obvious self-benefit.

○ **Honesty**: They will have an obvious **hidden agenda** and may also follow their own course of action rather than '**do what we say we will**', because their own course is perceived as leading to the desired position.

○ **Availability**: They will not always ensure **calls are returned**, since some will not advance their personal cause. They will be selective about allowing only those seen as potential allies access under '**you can get to us**'.

○ **Professionalism**: They will not **focus** on the company's objectives and priorities, concentrating, instead, on trivia, politics and their own agenda.

Once you have had this discussion you can move to Step 3.

Step 3: Action plan

Ask the individual concerned to draw up an action plan to deal with the gap, using thinking techniques. You can then monitor the plan through Section One of the Groundrules Review. Understand that the process may take time so patience will be needed.

The Powerbase model summarizes the principal tools used by leaders to attract and keep followers. However, there are certain important underlying characteristics which move the leader into the 'meta leader' category. Again, any of these, if missing, can be developed if the individual has sufficient will to do so.

RECOGNIZING THE CHARACTERISTICS OF A META LEADER

1   Meta leaders are **visionaries**. They see things which, when articulated, are often obvious to all. This comes through their ability to hover like the kestrel and see the whole picture, not just what is in front of them. Having seen the whole picture they focus on their vision and aim for it but, if they receive new data, they are courageous enough to change, or to select a new vision or a new way of achieving the original vision. In brief, they see the unseeable, think the unthinkable and say the unsayable.

2   Meta leaders can **follow**. They understand and expect followers to have ideas as well. Because they are focused on winning, if they have to follow for a while to do so, they will.

3   Meta leaders believe that they and their company can **achieve** anything they set their minds to.

4   Above all, meta leaders **believe in themselves**. After all, if you don't believe in yourself no one else will.

Meta leaders believe that if they think they will lose, they definitely will. If they think they will win, then, in all probability, they will.

5   Meta leaders are **daydreamers** and proud of it. They spend a great deal of time just looking out of the window or doodling or just mentally exploring the planets. They have the capacity to think constantly. This often brings out their eccentric side.

I once found myself in a new position of seniority over a particular group of people, some of whom I knew did not think I had any right to be 'Head Honcho'. After a couple of days spent information-gathering and reading personnel files I called the group together.

I knew the meeting would be potentially difficult, given the views of some present. I resolved to tackle the problem head-on and, having looked at their personnel files, I had a measure (albeit a small one) of the characters involved. I asked the group to be in the Boardroom at a particular time. I was there early. This had two advantages: first, they could not 'group' before I arrived; and, second, I could observe their individual responses to the view which greeted them as they entered the room.

This view was of a large, oblong, 30-seater Board table. I sat at one end. The only other 'occupant' was a large sod of turf, ordered by me earlier that day from the groundstaff and placed, precisely, in the middle of the table. When the group were settled in their chairs I proceeded to ask each individual, in turn, what they saw on the table.

Their 'views' ranged from 'a sod' to 'some grass with soil under' to 'some grass and soil with worms in it'. When each person had given their views, I told them what I saw – 'two pints of gold top (milk)'. I went on to explain that what I saw was not only what **was** but what **could be**.

This sod made me think of a warm sunny day with fluffy clouds. I imagined I was picnicking in a huge field, making pictures from the clouds. I was, of course, with a beautiful woman and, as we dozed lightly, we were awoken by a milk cow which was eating our picnic.

My first instinct was, of course, to wish the cow dead and I imagined some steak. Being a vegetarian, however, this mood passed and instead I pondered on the irony of the cow eating a cake made from dairy products – re-engineering back to two pints of gold top!

The point was that my wider, deeper view of what was before me was more likely to take the company forward than some others. From that day on, daydreaming was accepted practice, with some real success stories in the creative area. Of course, initially, there was some healthy scepticism. But, gradually, as those who daydreamed began to practise their ideas and show how this generated positive advantages, that scepticism disappeared.

6   Meta leaders are **courageous**. They are prepared to take risks and to let others take risks on their behalf (now, that **is** brave!). They recognize that they and others must, and will, make mistakes. They see lack of mistakes as **lack of decisions**.

Risk has been a constant feature in my own life – from leaving Liverpool to changing jobs as often as I have, to climbing mountains and skiing to the magnetic North Pole to setting up my own company. I have no doubt that I will take many more. The point is that I know, from experience, that without risk there is no real progress.

This is not to say that you cannot survive in a top role without allowing others to grow through taking risks. You will all be familiar with senior people who walk right down the middle, possibly playing corporate politics or consistently justifying why they have not empowered others. They are in the 'me too' group. Lower down the organization you find 'job's worth' managers and staff who perceive that it's safe **not** to make decisions. They are not leaders. Meta leaders pay no more attention to change than they do their own breathing. It's just something which happens when they are around.

Constant change is a way of life. Consider how you evolve as a human being – you are not the same person at 40 that you were at 16.

7   Meta leaders are **passionate** about their subject, company, product – whatever they are talking about. This breeds a belief among their followers that the leader is worthy of the position. There is nothing more demoralizing than having a middle-of-the-road approach to winning.

Even if the leader has consulted all concerned and drawn up a good business strategy or short-term sales target, if they delivered their vision in a dispassionate monotone, their followers will not believe it is achievable. If the leader doesn't seem to care, why should anyone else?

If, however, followers are made to feel that this incredibly tough strategy is achievable by the passionate way the leader talks about it, they will want to achieve it as much as they do.

8   Meta leaders **love people**. They are not threatened when they see someone grow – they welcome it. They see the value of having good people following them.

This love and trust of others allows them to ask people questions. Although, the traditional perception has tended to be that leaders 'should know' and not need to ask, today's meta leader sees it differently. Continuously asking questions means continuously learning. If the leader does this it encourages others to do the same and prevents vital information being lost.

9   Meta leaders naturally **develop themselves**. They are aware that to become a leader is one thing, but to stay in that position is another. It requires constant development and soul-searching. Being honest with themselves is important. I know numerous Directors who believe that they do not need development.

10   Meta leaders continually work on their **communication skills**, recognizing that all the good ideas in the world won't work unless you communicate them effectively.

I was taught this profound lesson about the importance of asking questions by my son, Martin, who, at the time, was about five years old. One day Martin was standing by our pond. When I saw him I thought he looked sad, although I could only see his back. I wandered over. When I drew nearer I found out what he was looking at – a dead fish floating on the surface of the pond.

I felt I needed to say something profound. I said, 'God wants it.'

Martin looked up at me and asked, 'What does God want with a dead fish?'

Having dug the first hole, I dug some more. 'It wasn't dead when He wanted it.'

'What?', screamed Martin, 'Did He kill it just so He could have it?'

'Go and get your football,' I said.

Ten minutes later I asked him what he had been thinking about while looking at the dead fish. He replied, 'I was trying to work out how to catch it, so I could give it to the cats!'

If I had only asked a question, instead of making a statement, I would not have exposed my son to the belief that he now holds that God is selfish!

STYLES OF LEADERSHIP

Having identified the key characteristics of leadership it is worth considering the different ways in which these characteristics are put into practice through differing leadership styles.

The illustration above visually symbolizes the three main 'staging posts' of leadership ranging from dictator through autocrat to democrat. However, the meta leader is not an autocrat, a democrat or dictator, but a mixture of all three. This mix varies for different problems or opportunities. What is important is that the leader knows which style to use at any one time.

Someone who continuously dictates will not encourage, so their team will not follow all the time. A consistent democrat will not be the dynamic shaper that followers are looking for. Too much of one style will inevitably lead to failure.

Should the leader make decisions based on emotion or data? There is no hard and fast rule but, on balance, most dynamic people I know lean towards emotion or intuition. This is not a 'better' way, just a different one.

KNOWLEDGE BASE (OR 'I KNOW A MAN WHO CAN...')

So far, we have discussed leadership in terms which relate very much to 'who you are'. There is another element which is also important – 'what you know' or, more importantly, 'what should you know?' as a leader.

Many people at top management level are afraid to admit that they do not know the answer. As a result, they make decisions when they are not in the best position to do so. It follows that many of those decisions create unsuccessful outcomes – as well as frustration for those that 'did know' and were not asked. This is especially true when those that knew find themselves clearing up the mess!

One of the most powerful and motivating statements that a leader can make is '**I don't know, what do you think?**'. The view that not to know everything is a sign of weakness is so wrong.

Those who profess to know everything will inevitably proceed to do everything – frustrating all those around them. The 'I'll do it myself; I'm the only one I can trust' leader is then surprised to discover a 'lack of ownership' in their company when things go wrong. After all, employees working for this sort of manager might be forgiven for thinking 'Why should I take ownership of problems which were created by your lack of willingness to empower me in the first place?'.

As you climb a structured ladder to a position in which others report to you, you may have to change your approach. Your role may now mean more coordinating, organizing, motivating and mentoring.

I developed the following model to help me identify and check for myself at what level in an organization the specialist knowledge (whether product or subject – for example, accounts) should be located. I call it the 'Circle of Knowledge'.

THE CIRCLE OF KNOWLEDGE

The following exercise will help you to establish where the specialist knowledge base in your company currently rests. For the sake of the example, the assumption is that your company has a Principal (you), with six Senior Executives. Each executive has some key operating executives reporting to them.

The first step is to draw a circle and put your name in the circle. Then on a separate piece of paper, list the functions that the Senior Executives have, and give yourself marks out of 10 for each of those functions. For example, look at sales. When scoring yourself you may consider that you are quite knowledgeable about that and award yourself 8 out of 10. For finance you may score 6 and for legal knowledge you may give yourself 4

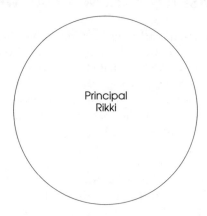

points. Follow the process through and calculate your average score. Write this average score in the circle with your name and position.

Now, draw another circle around the first one and write 'Senior Executives' in it. On a separate piece of paper write the separate functions that each of your Senior Executives covers. For example, sales might cover retail, industrial and so on. Then mark the Senior Executives on each of their directions. For example, they may have a retail background so may score 9 on retail but may score only 4 on industrial. Average these scores.

When you have marked each Senior Executive take the overall average and put the number in the circle with 'Senior Executives' on it. You should now have two circles, Principal and Senior Executives, both with numbers on.

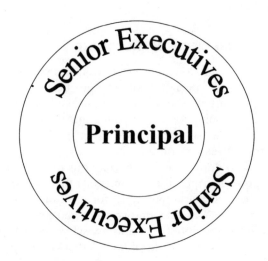

Follow the same process for your Key Operating Executives. Again, take their subsections to mark against. Management accounts, for example, might consist of monthly accounts, asset management, auditing and so on. Having marked each subsection and averaged the scores, calculate the overall average score for your Key Operating Executives. Then, draw a circle, outside the Senior Executives' circle, showing this average score. You should now have three circles: Principal, Senior Executives and Key Operating Executives, each marked with a score.

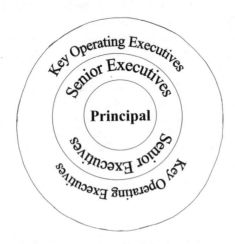

This exercise was done at BPFL at the end of the Thinking Organization development programme. I scored 7 as a Principal. My Senior Executives scored 8 and my Key Operating Executives 9. I didn't go all the way down and mark every member of staff, but I'll bet they'd have got 10s because, at the bottom of an organization, the requirement for an employee to be a specialist in their subject is likely to be greater. For a start, they do not have others reporting to them, so their jobs do not encompass a requirement to directly manage people.

If you compare this to a company run by a 'I must know it all' leader as described earlier, you will see that there will be a fundamental difference in the way they are run.

The BPFL circle showed that both its specialist knowledge base and its generalist knowledge base were located where they needed to be. If the balance is reversed, the company will be totally driven from the top, not only strategically – which is correct – but also in its day-to-day running. This seriously impedes progress in two ways:

1   It is impossible for one person to be an 'expert' in every area.
2   The sheer amount of time spent 'doing' – making decisions for everyone – reduces quality thinking time to practically nil.

As a result, not only does no one have time to think about the future at all, but empowerment is hindered on a day-to-day basis. If those at the top of organizations give out the message that they are the only ones capable of doing any job – however small – you create a situation of disempowerment. Those who should be making decisions don't bother because they know that the person at the top will take over. Equally, the person at the top walks around saying 'The only one who'll make a decision around here is me'.

The Circle of Knowledge methodology can be used at any organizational level. For example, a manager could place 'Manager' in the middle of the circle and use the outer circles for 'supervisor', 'assistant' and so on. You can even use the system if, like many, you employ temporary staff or when assessing the value of outsourcing.

If your current job is as a Principal, you cannot be a technical specialist in all areas. Having achieved this most senior position you must become a generalist. You may be able to keep up-to-date in your previous speciality if it is of a technical nature, but the reality is that you are now a generalist and must act out that role. Even a leading barrister now has others reporting to them, thus changing their role from specialists to specialist and generalist. To assume you are a specialist in all areas of the larger role would be a mistake.

DEVELOPING OTHERS THROUGH MENTORING

Having understood that leaders are made as well as born, having learned how to identify gaps in the powerbase and how to fill them, and having also learned how to use the Circle of Knowledge to assist in letting go (empowerment) and to help personal growth into any new job, it is now time to consider another key leadership tool. This one helps to get the best out of others – mentoring.

Primarily, mentoring means listening and offering thought processes as solutions. It is not offering solutions in themselves. These must be found by the individual being mentored – whom I have called the 'mentee'.

Mentoring can cover most areas, even if little or no knowledge exists on the mentor's part. This is because the mentor does not profess to know the answer, but is adept at asking the right question.

Socrates was one of the best mentors there has ever been and is probably one of the most widely known. He was renowned for asking probing questions which would cause students to give the answer that he (Socrates) knew was right. Socrates believed that the individual always had the answer. As a mentor, he guided them to the knowledge that was already there – allowing thought processes to follow their natural route.

For the process to work, the mentee must, of course, want to be mentored. A reluctant participant won't prepare for the sessions; they will have few ideas to discuss and most of those will be 'whinges'. Therefore the mentor has to make it clear that they are not there to solve problems, but to help the mentee find their own solutions.

Emphasis should be put on preparation. If the mentee has not prepared, both parties are wasting valuable time.

EXAMPLE OF MENTORING AGENDA

1   Review of personal objectives
2   Review of actions taken arising from previous session
3   Discussion of problems/current issues (work or non-work)
4   Review of techniques' / days' / Thinking Organization progress
5   Conclusion/summary

Choose the correct environment for the mentoring session to take place. It is difficult enough to open up – to do so in uncomfortable surroundings, with a telephone ringing is even worse!

There should, ideally, be no interruptions. Quite apart from being unprofessional, it conveys an impression of a lack of commitment on the part of the mentor.

Confidentiality is, of course, key. You may find that it takes some time to convince the mentee that you will not betray their confidences. The mentee may also need some time to become comfortable with being honest, so it is important, at the early stages, to give a great deal of encouragement.

When you are mentoring more than one person it is useful to gain anonymous feedback on your style. The key advantage is that, as mentor, you quickly find out if your style is good enough or needs modifying.

Mentoring on the move

When I was involved in marketing management for a petrol company, I wanted to persuade one of the site operators that he should change the way he ran his site. It was his site, however, so, although I could have used the heavy-handed 'contract' approach this would have taken too long and would not have changed the operator's outlook. So one day I asked him just to sit in the car with me while we went and looked at some competitor sites. We parked outside the first one and I said, 'Right, all we're going to do is sit here, watch and take the mickey out of the site.' I let him do most of the mickey-taking. We then did this at several more sites – looking at the dirty pumps, the badly placed signs, the operators ignoring customers, etc. Then I drove him back, parked over the road from his own site and watched. I didn't have to say anything!

One 'tool' which can help mentoring is a motivation questionnaire. Looking at the results of this type of questionnaire helps the mentor explore individual 'drivers' with each mentee. This, in turn, allows effective discussions around:

○   where the mentee is
○   what motivates them
○   what needs doing and how.

A common motivator is 'fear of failure'. I have already expressed the view that 'failure' is not an acceptable term for me, and should be replaced by 'losing'. The only reason I use it here is that it is used on many particular questionnaires. If this particular motivator is scored highly on the questionnaire then, as a mentor, emphasize that not only is it **OK to lose**, but that it is **necessary in order to win**. Helping the mentee understand this point removes a great deal of pressure, increases confidence in decision-making and, inevitably, increases the 'win' to 'lose' ratio.

Mentoring is a way of making mentees realize their own potential by helping them understand that:

○   they know more than they think
○   they can learn as much as they can dream.

CONCLUSION

This chapter has provided important data on understanding the nature of leadership itself and the characteristics needed by those who wish to become meta leaders. There are situations, however, where leaders believe that they display these characteristics but their followers take a different view. In other words, the perceptions of the leader and their followers differ. In fact, perception plays a crucial role in determining whether a leader actually has any followers! This aspect is explored in the next chapter.

9

PERCEPTION RULES!

 Once upon a time a snail was lying on its side in a hospital bed. Along came the doctor, who was a badger. The badger said, 'You don't look at all well. What happened to you?'

The snail, rather woefully, relayed his story.

'It all began' he said 'when I was trying to cross a road. I remembered that I should look left and right and did so for two hours. During that time the coast was clear, so I set off. No sooner had I got on to the road when, out of nowhere, moving at tremendous speed comes this tortoise – and runs me over!'

Our own perception may be that a tortoise is slow – but maybe that's not the case from the snail's-eye view!

Time is often wasted because people misunderstand a comment, intention or action, not to mention the emotional upset that can occur because two people have a different understanding of the same word.

Part of creating a thinking organization is helping people consider their impact on others. Often we do not understand that someone else's perception of an issue is different from our own nor that they may not perceive us as we see ourselves. Given that perception equals reality (in the eyes of the perceiver, anyway), we must consider how to change others' perception of us so that it accords with the image we wish to convey.

Source: T Buzan with B Buzan (1995), *The Mind Map Book: Radiant Thinking,* **London: BBC Books**

If you want to see how different individual interpretations can be if everyone is left to their own devises, try this simple exercise – another 'Buzan original'!

With any group of people, take one word – for example, 'happiness' – then ask them to write it in the middle of a piece of paper, circle it and draw ten lines off the circle (see below). Give them one minute to write a word on each line, and then compare them. It is extremely unusual for any word on one person's piece of paper to exactly match that on another's. Even if one has 'Mum' and another has 'Mother' this is not the same interpretation of the concept.

If you have someone with a mischievous streak in the group it can also provide some interesting discussions! I once worked with a group in which one member, knowing how devoted another was to his wife, and that her name would inevitably be one of his words, also put that name down!

To change another's perception of me I have to recognize:

O   the need to work on changing that perception

and

O   that a change in perception can be achieved.

I have to grasp the simple fact that, for that other person, **perception is reality**.

TACKLING 'THE NEED'

One system that can help in this process is the Perspectives peer rating system (see the Appendix to this chapter) developed and produced by Saville & Holdsworth. It is based on their OPQ (Occupational Personality Questionnaire), which is a 'self-report' questionnaire. This means that you obtain the participants' view of themselves against a number of important areas – Relationships with People, Thinking Style, and Feelings and Emotions. The questionnaire then allows views on the same areas to be expressed by others – their manager, some peers and some direct subordinates.

Peer feedback is best given on an anonymous and/or averaged basis. If it isn't, you become drawn into defensive debates along the lines of 'I know he thinks that, but he's wrong'. Having said that, one of the ways in which you know that the Groundrules are facilitating open and honest feedback is when participants, after a time, feel free to discuss their ratings of each other.

With the Perspectives questionnaire each person ends up with a profile showing a number of lines on it – for example, one showing their view of themselves, plus their manager's view, that of their peers and that of those who work directly for them.

I have also seen the system work well when a team – for example, the Senior Executives of a company – all rate each other and the Principal also rates each one. The average of the Senior Executives is given as the 'peer' line. This may not be statistically pure but it works for the purpose in hand. It is important to make sure that the leader participates in the process, because this helps to create an environment where honest feedback is seen as the norm.

A profile like this provides the base information to stimulate each individual into seeing the potential need for change – in other words, to close the gap between others' perception and their own view if they choose to do so. However, consideration must be given to the way in which that information is used with each individual. This has to be on an individual basis and, typically, should take a minimum two sessions. The first session should be with someone trained in feeding back the questionnaire and the second part as a mentoring session as outlined earlier in Chapter 8. In both cases, the individual should be allowed as much time as necessary. Typically, each session will last two to three hours, but could take longer. Consequently, the process is time-consuming, and preparation for this is important.

Because the profile is visual it is a very powerful way of showing individuals the gaps that exist between their view of themselves and others' views of them. Often the manager and peer(s) have a broadly similar view of the person being rated, and it is this joint view that will differ from that of the individual being assessed. This is a fairly obvious point, really, since it is difficult for most of us to consistently present different faces to the world. If you are someone with a 'hidden agenda', then this is likely to be perceived by most of those who come into contact with you.

It can be difficult for people when they see the chasms between their own self-perception and the other views shown. You must keep reiterating that the purpose of the discussion is not to agree whose 'line' is 'right' – the truth is that there is no 'right' line – but to demonstrate the gaps in perception.

One of the scales on the questionnaire is 'caring'. Sometimes people can become quite emotional when they find out that others have marked them low on 'caring' whereas they have marked themselves quite highly. It is easy to take this measurement personally – participants can mistakenly believe that they are being judged as a 'bad person' by those who are rating them. Part of the feedback discussion here would then typically be:

○   'Does it matter if I'm seen as caring or not?'
○   'If so, how would someone have formed the view that I am uncaring?'

The individual would then go on to consider their behaviour: 'Is it the case that the only time they lunch with me, for example, I do nothing but moan about my employees, saying they are useless?'; 'Do they know so little about me as a person that they have no idea of the hours I spend visiting my old Granny?' Of course, once the individual begins to look for the reasons behind others' perceptions, they are well on the way to considering how they need to behave in order to create the perception they want.

DEMONSTRATING CHANGES IN PERCEPTION

It is very rewarding to see people suddenly grasp the point that achieving a change in perception has nothing to do with being a 'good' or 'bad' person but means closing a gap between how they see themselves and how others see them. This means that any change sought is just for the purpose of closing that gap – it does not mean making a fundamental personality change.

This realization allows discussions on behaviour to take place in a non-judgemental way and gives ownership of any course of action to the person most involved. Using the 'caring' example quoted earlier, the following questions could be discussed:

○   'Do you care enough about the difference in perception to do anything about it?'

O   'What impact could it be having on your relationships?'

O   'What could *you* do?'

This whole process links in with other elements of the Thinking Organization because the act of working through the profiles described on a personal basis starts to build the relationships that are then strengthened through the Groundrules Review. Each element is complementary, personal and interpersonal.

THE GROUNDRULES

Once people understand that individual perception is a reality it allows you to hammer home the point that **visibly** living the Groundrules is the key to both individual and organizational success. **What you are seen to do** creates the **perception** which creates the **reality**.

CONCLUSION

Having decided that others' perception of us is different from our own and that we may want to change that perception we need to understand what change is and why some seem to resist it. The next chapter explores this issue.

APPENDIX: EXAMPLES OF PERSPECTIVES AND MOTIVATION QUESTIONNAIRES

The following pages are reproduced with kind permission of Saville & Holdsworth Ltd.

motivation

PROFILE CHART
MQ.M5

Name

Date of testing

SHL®

Saville & Holdsworth Ltd

motivation

MQ.M5

NORM GROUP
MANAGERIAL & PROFESSIONAL (1992)
n = 487

Scale	Low (STENS)	1	2	3	4	5	6	7	8	9	10	High (STENS)
												ENERGY & DYNAMISM
E1	Takes time over tasks, works best without pressure. Demotivated by being rushed.	8-17	18-20	21-22	23-25	26-27	28-30	31-32	33-35	36-37	38-40	**Level of activity** — Invests energy readily. Thrives on time pressure. Always on the go. Pushes to get things done.
E2	Seeks moderate rather than extreme challenges. Targets not a major issue.	8-27	28-29	30	31-32	33-34	35	36-37	38-39	40		**Achievement** — Needs to achieve targets. Strives to overcome difficult challenges.
E3	Finds competitive environments uncongenial, even demotivating. Outperforming others is not a motivator.	8-20	21-22	23-24	25-27	28-29	30-31	32-33	34-35	36-37	38-40	**Competition** — Tries to do better than others. Comparison often spurs performance.
E4	Switches off rather than increasing effort when faced with failure or criticism.	8	9-12	13-15	16-19	20-22	23-26	27-29	30-32	33-36	37-40	**Fear of failure** — Needs to succeed to maintain self-esteem. Prospect of failure spurs activity.
E5	Does not seek out positions of power, influence or authority.	8-23	24	25-26	27-28	29-30	31-32	33-34	35-36	37-38	39-40	**Power** — Needs scope to influence and exercise authority. Demotivated when not given responsibility.
E6	Demotivated by intrusion of work requirements into personal life.	8-12	13-14	15-17	18-19	20-21	22-23	24-25	26-27	28-29	30-40	**Immersion** — Thrives on feeling involved. Invests energy in job. Prepared to work extended hours.
E7	Demotivated by over emphasis on profits and finance.	8-17	18-20	21-22	23-25	26-27	28-29	30-32	33-34	35-36	37-40	**Commercial outlook** — Likes creating wealth and profits. Demotivated when work not linked with cash value.
												SYNERGY
S1	Limited need for interaction with others.	8-25	26	27-28	29	30-31	32-33	34	35-36	37	38-40	**Affiliation** — Thrives on meeting people, harmonious team work and helping others.
S2	Has less need for recognition than most. Praise and congratulations not prime motivators.	8-26	27-28	29-30	31	32-33	34-35	36	37-38	39	40	**Recognition** — Likes good work to be noticed and achievements recognised. Becomes demotivated without support.
S3	Unconcerned about moral and ethical issues or quality of work.	8-25	26	27-28	29-30	31	32-33	34-35	36	37-38	39-40	**Personal principles** — Needs to feel that the organisation's work is sound. Demotivated when asked to compromise ethical standards.
S4	Not overly concerned by an element of risk. Does not mind inconvenience.	8-24	25-26	27	28-29	30	31-32	33	34-35	36-37	38-40	**Ease and security** — Needs to feel secure about job and position. Does not easily tolerate unpleasant conditions.
S5	Not spurred by opportunities for new learning and self development.	8-27	28	29-30	31	32-33	34	35	36-37	38	39-40	**Personal growth** — Motivated by work which provides opportunities for development, and acquisition of new skills.
												INTRINSIC
I1	Not greatly affected by degree of interest or variety in work.	8-28	29	30-31	32-33	34	35-36	37	38-39	40		**Interest** — Values stimulating, varied or creative work. Demotivated by too many run of the mill tasks.
I2	Motivated by existence of clear work systems and structures. Intolerant of ambiguity.	8-11	12-14	15-16	17-18	19-20	21-22	23-24	25-27	28-29	30-40	**Flexibility** — Favours a fluid environment without imposed structure. High tolerance of ambiguity.
I3	Amenable to guidance and supervision from above.	8-26	27-28	29	30-31	32-33	34	35-36	37-38	39	40	**Autonomy** — Needs to work independently, organise own approach. Demotivated by close supervision.
												EXTRINSIC
X1	Less concerned with having financial benefits linked to the job.	8-24	25	26-27	28-29	30	31-32	33	34-35	36-37	38-40	**Material reward** — Links salary, perks and bonuses to success. Demotivated when remuneration is perceived as unfair or poor.
X2	Less driven to seek advancement. Promotion prospects not important.	8-25	26-27	28-29	30-31	32-33	34-35	36	37-38	39	40	**Progression** — Career progress and just advancement are motivating. Slow promotion is demotivating.
X3	Relatively unconcerned with issues of rank and position. Status symbols unimportant.	8-23	24-25	26-27	28	29-30	31-32	33-34	35-36	37	38-40	**Status** — Concerned with position and status. Demotivated by lack of respect from others.
PERCENTILES		1	4	11	23	40	60	77	89	96	99	

SCALE A B A+B SS

motivation

MQ.M5

NORM GROUP

Group	Code	High description	Low description
ENERGY & DYNAMISM	E1	**Level of activity** — Invests energy readily. Thrives on time pressure. Always on the go. Pushes to get things done.	Takes time over tasks, works best without pressure. Demotivated by being rushed.
	E2	**Achievement** — Needs to achieve targets. Strives to overcome difficult challenges.	Seeks moderate rather than extreme challenges. Targets not a major issue.
	E3	**Competition** — Tries to do better than others. Comparison often spurs performance.	Finds competitive environments uncongenial, even demotivating. Outperforming others is not a motivator.
	E4	**Fear of failure** — Needs to succeed to maintain self-esteem. Prospect of failure spurs activity.	Switches off rather than increasing effort when faced with failure or criticism.
	E5	**Power** — Needs scope to influence and exercise authority. Demotivated when not given responsibility.	Does not seek out positions of power, influence or authority.
	E6	**Immersion** — Thrives on feeling involved. Invests energy in job. Prepared to work extended hours.	Demotivated by intrusion of work requirements into personal life.
	E7	**Commercial outlook** — Likes creating wealth and profits. Demotivated when work not linked with cash value.	Demotivated by over emphasis on profits and finance.
SYNERGY	S1	**Affiliation** — Thrives on meeting people, harmonious team work and helping others.	Limited need for interaction with others.
	S2	**Recognition** — Likes good work to be noticed and achievements recognised. Becomes demotivated without support.	Has less need for recognition than most. Praise and congratulations not prime motivators.
	S3	**Personal principles** — Needs to feel that the organisation's work is sound. Demotivated when asked to compromise ethical standards.	Unconcerned about moral and ethical issues of quality of work.
	S4	**Ease and security** — Needs to feel secure about job and position. Does not easily tolerate unpleasant conditions.	Not overly concerned by an element of risk. Does not mind inconvenience.
	S5	**Personal growth** — Motivated by work which provides opportunities for development, and acquisition of new skills.	Not spurred by opportunities for new learning and self development.
INTRINSIC	I1	**Interest** — Values stimulating, varied or creative work. Demotivated by too many of the mill tasks.	Not greatly affected by degree of interest or variety in work.
	I2	**Flexibility** — Favours a fluid environment without imposed structure. High tolerance of ambiguity.	Motivated by existence of clear work systems and structures. Intolerant of ambiguity.
	I3	**Autonomy** — Needs to work independently, organise own approach. Demotivated by close supervision.	Amenable to guidance and supervision from above.
EXTRINSIC	X1	**Material reward** — Links salary, perks and bonuses to success. Demotivated when remuneration is perceived as unfair or poor.	Less concerned with having financial benefits linked to the job.
	X2	**Progression** — Career progress and just advancement are motivating. Slow promotion is demotivating.	Less driven to seek advancement. Promotion prospects not important.
	X3	**Status** — Concerned with position and status. Demotivated by lack of respect from others.	Relatively unconcerned with issues of rank and position. Status symbols unimportant.

SCALE A   B   A+B   SS

STENS: 1   2   3   4   5   6   7   8   9   10

PERCENTILES: 1   4   11   23   40   60   77   89   96   99

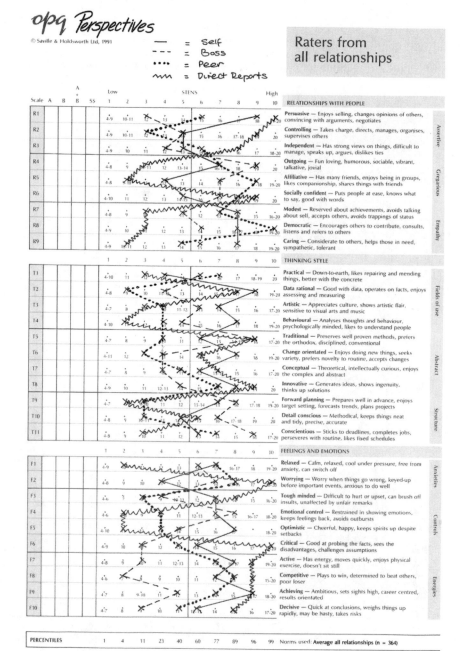

opq *Perspectives*
© Saville & Holdsworth Ltd, 1991

—— = Self
- - - = Boss
•••• = Peer
⌁⌁⌁ = Direct Reports

Raters from
all relationships

opq Perspectives

Scoring & Profile Charts

INDIVIDUAL BEING RATED

Last name

First name

Date

Age   Sex

Job title

Company

RATERS

Name	Relationship to person being rated
1	
2	
3	
4	
5	

Saville & Holdsworth Ltd, 1991
3 AC Court, High Street, Thames Ditton, Surrey, KT7 0SR

The reproduction of any part of this profile chart by duplicating
machine, photocopying process or any other method including
computer installations, is breaking the copyright law.
SHL and OPQ are registered trademarks of Saville & Holdsworth Ltd.

OP 2.5K 06/

10
CHANGE

❖

'**I need to change my company**' is amongst the most common statements made by Principals when asked what they need to do. Equally, if you talk to employees, customers, suppliers – anyone in a relationship with an organization – you will hear phrases like 'the company needs changing' or 'someone needs to do something about that company'.

But what is meant by 'change the company'?

A definition of 'company', taken from Collins *Modern English Dictionary*, says that a company is 'a group of people gathered together for a common purpose'.

When we say **'change the company**' *we really mean* **'change the people**'.

Resistance to change could be as simple as the staff of a company understanding this point when the Senior Executive does not.

Consider the following. Saying 'I don't like the way the company is being run' could mean 'I don't like the way the Senior Executives run the company [people]'. Resistance is beginning to build. What is actually meant might be 'I don't like the processes by which the company operates'.

So, to **'change the company's profitability'** *really means to* **'change the way people think about the company's profitability'**.

In practice this means making sure everyone involved understands that 'changing profitability' begins with the whole company. It means the whole company starting to consider all the elements of profit in all their decisions. This could have a profound effect – for a start, everyone putting their mind 'on the job' – not just an elite few.

To **'change the company's profile'** *would be to* **'change how key people in that company are perceived by the outside world'**.

There are many examples that could illustrate this, but one that immediately springs to mind is Virgin. Richard Branson is perceived as dynamic, energetic, pragmatic, creative and so on and, as a result, his company (that is, his people) are perceived in the same way.

TYPES OF CHANGE

Some change you will instigate yourself and some can be imposed on you either by other people or by circumstances, environment and so forth.

The kind of change that you bring about yourself is often viewed more positively. The decision is yours and within your control – to diet or to change your hairstyle, for example. Reaction to imposed change tends to be less positive because you may not feel in control and will, perhaps, feel threatened.

So, if you create a 'change environment' in your company – in which change is the norm – individuals will feel in control. They will continually instigate changes and are therefore more likely to be positive. This, in turn, will make that environment more likely to be successful than one in which a series of 'change programmes' are introduced, one after the other. Programmes are more likely to be perceived as 'imposed' and generate a less positive response.

THE MAIN BARRIER TO CHANGE

The main barrier to change lies in the individual and is **fear** – fear of:

O   ridicule
O   loss of security
O   loss of status
O   not being able to fit in
O   not being able to do a new job
O   the 'unknown'
O   of failing.

Fear becomes the main barrier to change, first because people don't acknowledge its existence and, second, by concealing itself in many different types of behaviour. The following are some examples of ways in which fear can show itself:

O   sarcasm
O   refusing to cooperate
O   pretending to cooperate but undermining the change by bad-mouthing to others
O   saying 'I knew it wouldn't work'
O   not being supportive of those trying to change – 'You don't actually believe that stuff do you?'
O   looking for reasons why change will fail – 'We tried that before and it didn't work'
O   using 'lack of resources' as an excuse

REASONS WHY PEOPLE WANT TO, AND DO, CHANGE

The good news is that the human race by and large has a strong instinct for survival. To survive it needs to change. Some of us recognize and act on that earlier than others. Examples of reasons why people change are:

O   They can see that they need to in order to survive.
O   They can see personal gain or benefits – for example, more money, better security, more skills.
O   They don't like what they have, so anything else is better.
O   They enjoy learning new things.

The characteristics of those who initiate or welcome change are:

O   self-belief
O   risk-taking

O   openminded/curious
O   trusting of others
O   not afraid of losing
O   creative
O   a positive attitude.

You'll be able to see the links here to some of the characteristics described under the Employment Shield and of meta leaders.

Key to your preparatory thinking, when considering change, is the realization that every single person in your company falls into one of two categories. Either they will be for change or against it to a greater or lesser degree. Either they will be prepared to understand what their particular fear is and face it or they will not.

'Managing change' is therefore managing:

1   **people** who welcome change, using them to implement change and showing them the rewards of doing so

and

2   **people** who fear change.

(It's that **people** word again!)

THE TRANSITIONAL CURVE

A useful starting point is to ask all concerned in the change process to identify where they believe they would fit on the transitional curve (see Figure 10.1). This demonstrates a process which we go through when confronted with change. The curve shows seven stages and indicates how the individual sees their own level of competence at each of those stages. 'Competence', in this respect, can mean competence in a particular job or, outside the business environment, it can mean competence in handling or adjusting to a personal situation, such as, for example, becoming a parent or getting divorced.

Each stage is characterized by typical behaviour and, underlying that behaviour, there are emotions. Stress is always involved in change, even when that change is positive. Someone who understands the stages is less likely to 'get stuck' in one stage, which can lead to stress emerging later in life. Of course, some people may move rapidly through all stages – again, the individual, their general attitude to life and the extent to which the change is sought or imposed will all play a part in this.

To explain the basic principles, let's assume that we've introduced some radical changes in working practices and that our employees (who see the

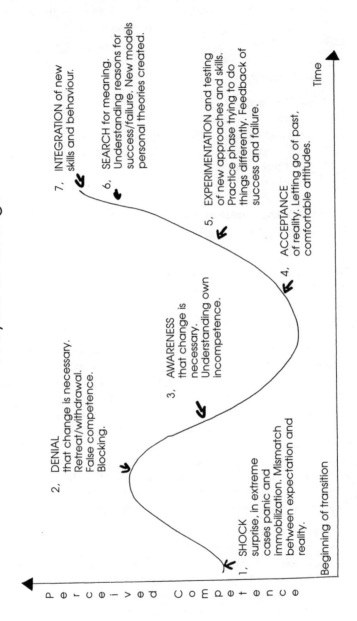

**THE TRANSITION CURVE
A cycle of change**

7, INTEGRATION of new
    skills and behaviour.

6, SEARCH for meaning.
    Understanding reasons for
    success/failure. New models
    personal theories created.

5, EXPERIMENTATION and testing
    of new approaches and skills.
    Practice phase trying to do
    things differently. Feedback of
    success and failure.

4, ACCEPTANCE
    of reality. Letting go of past,
    comfortable attitudes.

3, AWARENESS
    that change is
    necessary.
    Understanding own
    incompetence.

2, DENIAL
    that change is necessary.
    Retreat/withdrawal.
    False competence.
    Blocking.

1, SHOCK
    surprise, in extreme
    cases panic and
    immobilization. Mismatch
    between expectation and
    reality.

Beginning of transition

Perceived Competence

Time

Figure 10.1   The transitional curve

company as successful) are totally surprised that there is a need for a change in their jobs. In broad terms, the change is therefore seen as 'imposed', not as generated by those employees.

Initially, they enter ...

STAGE 1: SHOCK/SURPRISE

O   **Typical reactions:**
-   'I never knew that'
-   'This isn't the job I was employed to do'
-   'What do you mean I've got to learn computer skills?'

O   **Typical behaviour:**
-   unable to reason
-   freezing up

O   **Underlying emotions:**
-   fear (in this example about their ability to do the new job and what will happen if they don't)

After a time the 'news' sinks in and, for example, new job skills are outlined. The employees move to ...

STAGE 2: DENIAL

As can be seen in Figure 10.1, the curve rises into this stage, which, initially, may, seem a strange thing to do. However, if you remember that this represents the individual's – rather than others' – view of their own competence, it makes more sense. Depending on how extensive the change is, the denial stage is an essential part of the brain's survival mechanism. It is a way of making sure that the proposed change 'makes sense' – in a way it 'checks' that the change is really needed. There is only a problem when the denial stage persists too long or when the 'voice' in the individual's head continues to 'tell' them that the change is not needed. In an extreme case of denial, others will view the individual concerned as 'deluding themselves' about the 'reality' of their situation.

O   **Typical reactions:**
-   'I've done it this way for 20 years.'
-   'Keep your heads down, lads, they've done this kind of thing before and always come back to the old ways.'
-   'This is easy – can't see what the fuss was about.'
-   'It's not us that need to change, it's Finance.'

O   **Typical behaviour:**
-   going back to the 'comfort zone' (what I know I can do)
-   trivializing the importance of change

    – blaming others
O   **Underlying emotions:**
    – still fear – blocking
    – may actually 'feel' good – if you deny the need to change or blame someone else you no longer have to feel the fear

Assuming that individuals come through this stage, they gradually begin to recognize that what they do now is not good enough. Their perception of their own competence therefore starts to slide downwards. This is ...

STAGE 3: AWARENESS

At this stage, awareness refers to awareness of their own fear. It may be that they are still confused about the need to change.

O   **Typical reactions:**
    – 'I'm confused.'
    – 'What the **** is going on?'
    – 'This is so frustrating.'
O   **Typical behaviour:**
    – flatness in performance
    – aimlessness
O   **Underlying emotions:**
    – depression at realization of own incompetence
    – frustration at not knowing how to cope
    – feeling 'lost'

After Stage 3, things do start to look up! At Stage 4 the corner is turned ...

STAGE 4: ACCEPTANCE

This is a confidence-building stage: once something is accepted it is 50 per cent achieved.

O   **Typical reactions:**
    – 'Right, I'll look at where I am. This is what I want.'
    – 'Can someone round here help me go through this system again, so I can get it right?'
O   **Typical behaviour:**
    – visibly more prepared to experiment
    – letting go of the past and acceptance of 'what is' as the basis to build for the future
O   **Underlying emotions:**
    – relief at letting go
    – optimism for the future

By now, we're motoring on to …

STAGE 5: EXPERIMENTATION AND TESTING

Here, there is a degree of experimentation, but sometimes with a tendency to stereotype what 'should' happen.

O   **Typical reactions:**
  - 'We should be doing it this way.'
  - 'Let's try something different if that doesn't work.'

O   **Typical behaviour:**
  - a great deal of activity
  - possible conflict as frustration/anger emerges during testing

O   **Underlying emotions:**
  - excitement
  - anger
  - frustration

Now individuals begin to think about and 'internalize' the change. It starts to become their new natural 'way of doing'; they have moved to …

STAGE 6: SEARCH FOR MEANING

In this stage we begin to audit our thoughts and are more prepared to discuss with others what is going on.

O   **Typical reactions:**
  - 'How far do you think we've come?'
  - 'Do you think things are different now?'
  - 'How well do you think I'm doing?'

O   **Typical behaviour:**
  - withdrawal from activity in order to think
  - may talk to others about what's happening

O   **Underlying emotion:**
  - Calmer
  - feeling of control

STAGE 7: INTEGRATION

It is at this point that the individuals have changed the way they think and so changed the way they act. It is this 'real' change, which encompasses the 'whole' brain, including the emotions, which provides the means for realizing the potential for growth and development which arises from change.

The summary given above is, of necessity, a very brief description of a complex interplay of thoughts and emotions. For those interested in pursuing the topic in more depth, the following book can be recommended:

○   Rupert Eales-White (1994), *Creating Growth from Change: How you React, Develop and Grow*, London: McGraw Hill.

THE TRANSITIONAL CURVE AS A MANAGEMENT TOOL

It is important to ask at which stage each individual thinks they are and then test that. Except in obviously traumatic circumstances it is unusual to meet anyone who puts themselves at stages 1 or 2, and yet many are at those stages. With these people you must let them know that where they 'really' are is less important than 'where they want to be'.

What the transitional curve also does is emphasize the point made earlier that real change, whilst it **has to become a natural process, is unlikely to be an 'overnight' process**. The mere comprehension that something has changed in your life (which can be overnight) does not guarantee acceptance or internalization or consistent change in behaviour. This is why 'fad' management does not lead to any form of lasting or Stage 7 'integrated' change'.

THE ROLE OF THE LEADER IN CHANGE

The role of the leader is to give direction and create the right atmosphere for change to be seen in a positive light. If there is no leader of change it won't stop change happening. All it means is that the change will have no direction. You can't stop people changing because you cannot control all the forces acting on them.

Leaders also have to understand the process of change personally. Going through change and continuing to go through it yourself can only help you appreciate the work that is necessary for true change to happen. Here, as in so many other circumstances, a leader will inspire others to try by 'doing' as well as by 'saying'.

Personal example promotes willingness in others and means that the leader is in a better position to help others change. This produces concentrated effort and a better chance of achieving the change which is needed.

SUMMARY

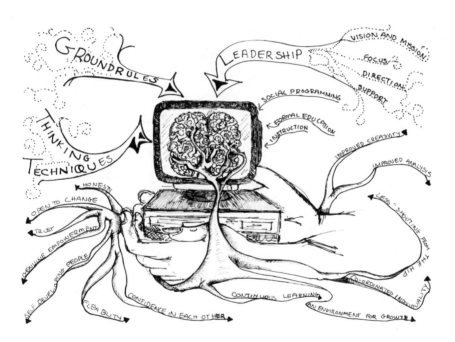

And finally – having added first the Groundrules (the culture), then the thinking techniques (the tools), we have added leadership (closing the sale). The resultant person and company now has the ability to harness (through the Groundrules), focus (using thinking techniques) and release (using leadership ability) the power (potential) that has always been there but which has been locked away.

The Thinking Organization:

○　　recognizes that leadership can be learned
○　　plugs gaps in the powerbases – knowledge, position, charisma and communication
○　　understands that part of the process of leadership is to become more of a generalist and accept that specialist knowledge can and should be held by others
○　　recognizes that there are many styles of leadership
○　　has mentoring as a key part of any personal and therefore organizational, development plan
○　　works on the basis that perception can be changed into *your* reality
○　　makes change natural and therefore does not have to 'overcome resistance'.

ACTION PLAN

1   Assess yourself against the **Powerbases**.

2   Assess your organization's knowledge base, using the **Circle of Knowledge**.

3   Obtain information on how you are perceived and consider what to do about the differences in others' view of you.

4   Consider what **you** mean by change, express it well and think about how you will make it natural.

REVIEW BY TONY BUZAN

LEADERSHIP

At the beginning the Chapter 8 Rikki makes a controversial, provocative and 'politically incorrect' claim: that people need leaders in part because we all need good role models and because 'at some point we all need to be given a direction in which to travel'. I am delighted to support his renegade views!

Research is increasingly demonstrating that the human brain not only needs to follow, it is **designed** to follow. This can be understood much more easily if we substitute the word 'follow' for the word 'mimic'. Consider for a moment everything you have learned simply by copying…

This point was most forcefully made by the great Japanese creative thinker and innovator in the field of music teaching, Senechi Suzuki. Suzuki had been experimenting with various methods of teaching people music, when he suddenly had a blinding realization: that every Japanese child learned to speak Japanese!

This 'blindingly obvious' realization contained within it intricate complexity and profound depth. What Suzuki had observed was that the brain of every human being on the planet (and that includes you, dear reader!) learns to play the most complicated musical instrument in the world – the vocal cords – by copying (following) role models.

If you think about this, what it means is that any baby (any brain) will learn any language to which it is exposed as long as it is allowed to 'follow the leader', whether that language be Japanese, Portuguese, Music-ese, Art-ese, Thinking-ese, Chinese, or Leadership-ese! Not only will the brain do this, it will do it perfectly. Thus you now speak your main language, in the way that those you followed do.

This positive learning experience proves incontrovertibly that you can learn anything to a higher degree of competency, provided that you are given the correct thinking and learning environment, the correct thinking and learning tools and the correct leaders and guides.

It also confirms that in order for there to be 'super-success' there had better be meta leaders!

Nurture allows **nature** *to express its full potential.*

In view of the above, the role of the meta leader can be seen as even more important than it had been thought to be. The characteristics outlined in *Creating a Thinking Organization* are ones that **every** leader needs to develop to the full.

From the brain's viewpoint, daydreaming is an especially significant skill and demands ongoing practice and development. Daydreaming requires engaging the 'imagination' facility from the 'right brain' and was one of the principal skills developed by the great leaders and geniuses from history.

Indeed, one of the greatest geniuses of all time, Albert Einstein, was, first, nearly expelled from academic institutions on account of his daydreaming and, second, achieved his high ranking in the portals of genius for using and developing that very same skill! When teaching his postgraduate students he insisted that, instead of concentrating on their standard studies, they played 'thinking games' in which they focused on a particular problem and devised structured daydreaming towards a solution to that problem.

As a small exercise for yourself, review the Thinking Organization and notice areas where the ability to daydream and imagine more effectively and magnificently will enhance your thinking and other processes.

Another characteristic of the great leaders and geniuses was their commitment to a lifetime of self-development and improvement. Alexander the Great, one of the great leaders of all time, used to study Homer and Aristotle incessantly while on his long military marches. He would intersperse these studies with jumping on and off chariots and horses in order to improve his strength, agility and speed.

In the fields of the arts and the sciences it is the same. The great artists and musicians consistently explored new knowledge and exploited new styles and techniques throughout their lives. It is reported, for example, that Michelangelo was furious when he realized that he was dying, stating that it was too early because he'd only just begun to understand what life was all about!

The lesson to be learned from all this is that, to be a great thinker and thus in order to be a great leader, you need to keep your thinking machine in increasingly good shape. Look after it in the same way as Rikki looks after his sons – **encourage**, **play and develop**.

PERCEPTION RULES

One can say in support of Rikki's thesis, **it does**! Your brain is the supreme biocomputer and operates on the principles of association and sensory imagination. The positions and the perspectives from which you view the world and the universe are, by definition, unique. Therefore, by definition, so is everyone else's. This means that **you** and **only you** will see things as you do. No matter what anyone else wants you to think or feel, what you actually do think and feel will be your 'truth'. Once you realize this basic 'truth', your understanding of yourself and others will improve in one great leap and your abilities as both leader and follower will be so enhanced that they will become almost automatic.

CHANGE

It is often thought that change is somewhat unnatural and somehow opposed to normal brain function. Nothing could be further from the truth.

The human brain is **designed** as a change mechanism. To survive it must constantly add new knowledge to its existing and vast databases in order to bring it up-to-date with reality and change its probability functions for survival in varying situations, thereby ensuring that its existence continues.

The patterns of thought laid down in the circuitry that dazzles between the brain cells are literally 'probabilities of recurrence'. What you think at any one moment increases the probability that you will think it again. And the more often that you think a thought the higher the probability that the thought will be repeated again. Those who survive and become leaders continually update their thought patterns, and, as they mature, make a habit of thinking in ways that allow them growing flexibility, adaptability and creativity, rather than repeating thought patterns and habits that lead to an ever increasing linearity, 'greyness', inflexibility and rigidity.

This latter point emphasizes that to lead and create you **must** take risks and that, in taking risks, you increase the probability of the occasional 'mistake' or 'failure'.

Without exception the great and towering leaders, intellects and geniuses throughout history relished their mistakes and took delight in learning from them, thus paving the way for the next great leap forward.

As Rikki has stressed, when we say '**change the company**' we really mean '**change the people**'.

The leader is in a state of constant change and encourages, allows others to follow their example and leads by example.

Like the brain, the leader is a change agent!

PART IV
THE THINKING ORGANIZATION IN PRACTICE

❖

INTRODUCTION TO PART IV

The main body of this book is now complete. I have described the principles behind the three integral parts needed to create a Thinking Organization.

1   Creating the environment
2   Thinking in the environment
3   Leading in the environment.

Here are some final thoughts on why the Thinking Organization wins.

1   **It works**. Once people experience how it feels to win they are hungry for more. Instant results happen – usually on a small scale – but even this creates an expectation of longer-term success, starting that self-perpetuating cycle.

2   **The Groundrules provide an important link to the outside world**. Most involved can see that living the Groundrules in everyday life helps how we see and treat each other.

3   **The results are visible**. In almost 100 per cent of cases others notice a difference in the attitude of those exposed to the environment/techniques. Typical quotes are 'my manager is happier', 'more relaxed', 'the department works better'.

4   **The individual gets personal results – personal benefit**. So many who have been exposed to the concept have achieved much more than they, or others, expected.

5   **The system is auditable**. The fact that clear targets are set at the outset and that there is a mechanism to check all along the way helps ensure success. This mechanism is the Groundrules Review which allows for relationships to be regularly audited, thus

avoiding build-up of frustration. The system is easy to use, provides a framework for honest feedback and is built totally around the individual.

6.   **It is simple**. All those who go through the process feel, instantly, that creating a Thinking Organization is achievable – it uses everyday language.

7.   **The thinking techniques give confidence to all those taught**. The realization that everyone can grow is a truly rewarding experience, freeing people from self-imposed limitations – they no longer believe that what they are is what they will always be.

8.   **The Thinking Organization channels the brain's natural ways of thinking**. The brain's purpose is to think, in the multiple senses of the word. An organization is a collection of brains. Much like the principle underlying many martial arts, the environment created by the Thinking Organization frees, channels and directs the power of these brains.

9.   **The fundamentally 'individual' approach to management within the Thinking Organization allows each member of that organization to feel genuinely recognized, trusted and, therefore, valued**. Individual style, preference and contributions are not merely tolerated, they are 'the norm'. People are trusted to work within the Groundrules and towards the vision and, as a result, grow to trust each other.

The acronym IOUCHAP was created by my finance manager in Burmah Petroleum Fuels Ltd. It is fitting, then, that I follow with another of his creations. This time it is a visual representation showing the differences between existing in an environment which does not implement the Thinking Organization techniques and one which does. It is based on a rainbow with a kestrel (seeing the big picture) on the one side and a dodo (looking at the ground) on the other.

All that remains now is to outline a detailed implementation plan to follow or adapt, and to let you read the thoughts of those who have been exposed to the concept. This is followed by a grand action points summary and a final review by Tony Buzan.

11

IMPLEMENTING THE PLAN

Outlined in this chapter is the approach taken to creating a Thinking Organization. As you would expect, its core components are:

○ teaching the Groundrules – to create the environment
○ teaching thinking techniques.

The length of time taken to implement the Groundrules will obviously vary depending on the number of employees in the company. The principles, however, remain the same. In addition, there are other elements which should, ideally, be included as they speed up the process.

The process detailed is based on a fictional company with a Principal, four Senior Executives, eight Key Operating Executives and a further 150 employees, some of whom are field-based.

The process is not described in chronological order since, in reality, many of the different areas covered (for example, thinking, leadership and so on) are carried out in parallel, as they are inextricably interconnected.

PROGRAMME FOR CREATING A THINKING ORGANIZATION

THE BOARD – THE PRINCIPAL AND SENIOR EXECUTIVES (4)

Content	Duration	Results
Planning Day	1 day	○ Agree employee groupings ○ Agree methods/content of communication about the process to employees ○ Agree timetable to suit 'life-cycle' of business ○ Agree which thinking techniques to teach
Thinking techniques	6 (individual) days	
Each day designed around teaching a technique and building one on another to combine them. Each applied to a specific and key company issue		○ Improved but focused creativity. ○ Clearer analysis ○ Improved cross-functional knowledge and working ○ Improved ability to ask questions and see 'the big picture'.
Leadership ○ What is it? (Whole) Board) ○ The Board as leaders (whole Board) ○ Strategic v. operational or 'thinking v. doing'	2 days	○ Use of Powerbase model identify leadership style/gaps and plan how to fill them ○ Clarification of roles (individual and collective) ○ Individual plans to get you from where you are to where you want to be; use of Circle of Knowledge

Cont'd

Content	Duration	Results
Vision and mission Do they exist? If not, work to create vision (with the Principal, using input from other Board members as necessary). If already in existence, how visual/memorable – redo if needed	1 day	○ 'Useable' vision and mission
Change ○ What is it? ○ Whose responsibility? ○ Understanding where change starts (with you)	1 day	○ Clearer understanding of nature of change ○ More realistic planning and expectations of others ○ Use of transitional curve

Followed by completion of personality questionnaires to provide information on how each Board member is perceived.

Content	Duration	Results
Individual assessments The completion of the questionnaires is followed by individual feedback sessions at time to suit. Average 2 hours each person.	1 day	Report containing feedback analysis and recommended actions for each Board member. Combined with the information from powerbase analysis, this provides an individual and collective development plan.
Groundrules ○ Detailed interpretation of the wording plus link to company examples. ○ Principles of the Groundrules Review	1 day	Complete understanding is the key to creating the environment, which will give you the following outputs: ○ empowerment ○ total quality ○ business process ○ re-engineering ○ customer service mentality (internal and external) ○ culture audit mechanism ○ quality assurance

Cont'd

Content	Duration	Results
		○ effective teamworking ○ consistent decisions ○ basis for integrated personnel strategy ○ relationship marketing ○ value chain analysis etc., etc. without the need for additional programmes
Groundrules Review follow-up Following each of the first two sets of reviews carried out by the Board, to look at: ○ Any misinterpretation ○ What happened ○ What worked ○ What didn't work ○ What to do	1 day	○ Increased understanding of the Groundrules and Groundrules Review process ○ Audits process consistency ○ Additional help if needed
Communication skills ○ Forms of communication ○ Problems: – listening – giving and receiving constructive feedback – handling conflict	1 day	Assists in moving quickly to gain maximum benefit from Groundrules Reviews
Mentoring skills ○ What skills are involved? ○ Practice ○ Planning sessions	1 day	○ Builds on communication ○ Supplements the individual reviews

Cont'd

Content	Duration	Results
Individual mentoring of the Board Individual sessions (3 half-day sessions each for each of the Senior Executives plus 4 half-days for Principal)	8 days (total)	○ Access to external and objective mentor ○ Experience of being mentored is the best way to ensure that skills are put into use further down the organization. ○ Reality not theory.

Total number of days for the Board: 24 (25 per cent thinking techniques)

KEY OPERATING EXECUTIVES (8)

Content	Duration	Results
Leadership/change As per Board, excluding work on vision	1 day	As per Board
Thinking techniques	6 individual days	As per Board
Individual assessments As per Board	2 days	As per Board
Groundrules As per Board	1 day	As per Board
Groundrules Review follow-up As per Board	2 days (2 half-day sessions for each of 2 groups)	As per Board
Communication skills As per Board	1 day	As per Board

Cont'd

Content	Duration	Results
Mentoring skills As per Board	1 day	As per Board
Individual mentoring As per Board	3 days (2 x 2hr sessions each)	As per Board

Total days for Key Operating Executives: 17 (35 per cent thinking techniques)

REMAINING EMPLOYEES (150)

Content	Duration	Results
Groundrules Based on 5 groups of 30–35 employees on a regional or other practical basis	5 days	As per Board and Key Operating Executives

Total days for employees: 5

The reason less time needs to be spent at this level of the organization is that, by now, the Principal, Senior Executives and Key Operating Executives are, first, living the Groundrules and the employees can therefore see how they should be living. Second, they are practising the thinking techniques and pushing them through the organization.

The total involvement on-site with the company, over 12 to 18 months, is:

Principal/Senior Executives	24
Key Operating Executives	17
Employees	5
Total	**46 days (26 per cent thinking techniques)**

The 46 days shown are, of course, only the tip of the iceberg. In between formal 'sessions' as, for example, in the typical 'thinking technique' day shown below, those involved would be working on their own development, on issues which arise as a result of mentoring or on live case studies which practise and reinforce the techniques.

TYPICAL AGENDA FOR INDIVIDUAL 'THINKING TECHNIQUES' DAY

08.30–11.10   Group working on case study and preparing to feedback on:

    ○ Content: conclusions, ideas, suggestions, etc. in response to the questions raised
    ○ Thinking process: how conclusions were reached, which ideas were discarded and why, critical incidents when the content or direction changed and why, etc

11.10–11.40   Group feedback/presentation on 1 and 2 above
11.40–13.00   Review:

    ○ Positive feedback on content – what we liked, found stimulating
    ○ Questions to the group to check understanding, seek clarification, challenge, explore thinking processes
    ○ Learning review

14.00–15.15   Exercise – developing a problem-solving framework:

    ○ Group work
    ○ Review

15.15–16.30   Belbin's team roles and team problem solving
16.30–18.00   Creativity and problem-solving techniques in context:

    ○ Overview – link to stages of problem-solving process
    ○ Brainstorming (revisited)/clustering
    ○ Force field analysis (FFA) – worked example

18.00–18.30   Case study briefing – 'Role of Area Sales Representative' apply FFA
18.30–18.40 Review, close and move to bar!

The main emphasis in terms of formally structured time is at the top of the organization. This is because, as has been stressed all the way through the book, it is those at the top who create the environment. Given that the key to creating this environment is the Groundrules, it is also crucial that each level is not allowed to 'pass them down' or judge the level below them until:

O   they are clear in the interpretation of the Groundrules

and

O   they are visibly living them.

This will usually take at least two or three live Groundrule Reviews. There are three-month intervals between Reviews, and you need two or three Reviews to really understand and live the Groundrules, so, the minimum time for 'passing down' is around nine months.

12

THE PAY-OFF

❖

A group of people whose organization started the Thinking Organization process in 1992 were surveyed five years later on what they thought about the programme now that they are no longer with that company. This data section gives the results of that survey.

SURVEY RESULTS

THE QUESTIONS ASKED:

1   How does your new employer's culture differ from that taught in the Thinking Organization?
2   Do you still use the Groundrules?
3   If yes, in what context (work/home)?
4   If no, what stopped you?
5   Do you use any of the thinking techniques?
6   For what do you use them?
7   Have you passed on your learning to anyone?
8   What has been their response?
9   Any other comments (they were asked for 'warts and all' views)

THE RESPONSES:

Q.1   How does your new employer's culture differ from that taught in the Thinking Organization?

Of those that had not set up their own company, 100 per cent said the culture in their new employment was not as dynamic or effective as in the Thinking Organization.

Some typical comments were as follows:

O   'Willing people but doing their own thing without liaison, communication or consideration for others.'

O   'Most predominantly there is a lack of team spirit, honesty and low ownership.'

O   'The style is very political. Protection of one's turf is important to many senior managers.'

O   'Don't really live their vision, they are No. 1 in their market but don't constantly try to improve.'

O   'Lacks clearly communicated vision.'

O   'Decision by committee, little accountability, negative attitudes, no ownership – creativity is a foreign culture.'

Comment: Janet Tapsell

The comments from those who have experienced the Thinking Organization and have now been 'relegated' into 'non-Thinking Organizations' show the impact on individuals that a leader makes when making the decision to implement the concepts in this book. Encouraging employees to open their minds, challenge themselves and act on individual and creative thinking in pursuit of a clearly understood vision creates employees who can never be satisfied in any other type of environment. Wherever they are they will look to re-create the dynamism and focus they have experienced. These are the 'dynamic and focused' employees that, in Personnel, we are asked to recruit … the ones supposedly in short supply … The comments show you they are not in short supply – they are everywhere, but waiting for those leaders who, rather than seeing 'dissatisfaction', understand the positive forces that drive it and use those forces to create a long term future.

Q.2   Do you still use the Groundrules?

All (100 per cent) of the respondents answered 'Yes' to this question.

Q.3   If yes, in what context?

O   'Wherever and whenever I can.'

O   'I used them to select my current employer.'

O   'It's like eating. You can't stop once you get the taste.'

O   'Managing myself, co-Directors, customers and family.'

O   'Work life and personal life.'

O   'Developing company and people within it.'

O   'All people interactions.'

O   'For evaluation of clients and associates.'

O   'In managing own team and personal life.'

O   'With my boss.'
O   'In everything I do, at work and socially.'
O   'Both Groundrules and thinking techniques have been used to
        good effect in my personal life.'

Q.4   If no, what stopped you?

Not applicable.

Q.5   Do you use any of the thinking techniques?

99.5 per cent said 'Yes'. Only one person said that they were not using any
of the techniques. Of the remainder, five techniques, in particular, were
popular.

Technique	Ranked preference
Mind Mapping®	1
Force field analysis	2
Six Thinking Hats	3
Brainstorming	4
SWOT	5

All of those using the thinking techniques used more than one. The
percentages of those actively using a particular technique are as follows:

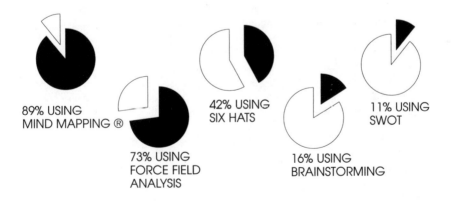

89% USING
MIND MAPPING ®

73% USING
FORCE FIELD
ANALYSIS

42% USING
SIX HATS

16% USING
BRAINSTORMING

11% USING
SWOT

Q.6   For what do you use them?

O   'Long-term problem solving.'
O   'Note-taking.'
O   'Idea generation.'
O   'Mind Mapping as a planning tool.'
O   'Brainstorming to get ideas out.'
O   'Mind Mapping for preparing reports and presentations.'
O   'Force field and SWOT to aid implementation.'
O   'Mind Maps for taking in lots of information quickly.'
O   'Six Thinking Hats to identify human reaction to change.'
O   'Mind Mapping for braindump on new ideas and presentations.'
O   'Force field to decide which option to take.'
O   'Six Hats to see if white hat answers are forthcoming.'
O   'Force field for challenging long held views.'
O   'Mind Mapping for agenda planning as well as preparing for Groundrules Reviews.'
O   'Prioritizing.'
O   'Strategy development.'
O   'Mind Mapping for acquisitions.'
O   'Personal development.'
O   'Job searching – Mind Mapping.'

Employee comments during the formal development programme

Combining creative thinking techniques with one to one mentoring is a combination which I have found very stimulating and thought provoking. The challenge for me has been to use the techniques that I find useful and blend these into everyday working practices. The mentoring allows an ongoing feedback process to develop, which has helped me become more self-aware and to experience consciously the benefits of the new approach. This process has, at times, been uncomfortable – as we have discussed other people's perceptions of our styles – but has, I believe, a great deal to offer.

Case studies based on business problems facing our company enabled us to learn realistically how the different techniques and models could be applied in day to day work. Thinking about how I can pass on the techniques and thinking processes to my team reinforces the learning process for me.

Q.7   Have you passed on your learning to anyone?

21% PASSING
ON TO FAMILY

74% PASSING
LEARNING ON

As can be seen above, 74 per cent said they were passing on learning, although 40 per cent of these said they were finding it difficult because of culture problems. Apart from colleagues, the next most popular recipient was the spouse – 21 per cent of respondents doing so! Others included children and participants on college courses.

Q.8   What has been their response?

O   'Generally positive with senior management.'
O   'Good – son uses techniques to help learning.'
O   'My wife is actually far more visual in Mind Mapping but the whole thinking process has changed our outlook on continuing education.'
O   'Very enthusiastic.'

Q.9   Any other comments?

O   'Network and companies growing.'
O   'The entire development programme was, I feel, highly beneficial. It has given me increased confidence in employment and in my personal life.'
O   'Have set up a system of mentoring of both business and social contacts for joint development work.'
O   'The two years spent on the programme were the most productive of my working life. Changed both my general outlook and ability to think outside the box.'
O   'I feel I am going to explode with frustration. Can we create what we had again – please, please, please?!'
O   'It raises your expectation of yourself and others.'
O   'The development programme enabled me to be much more confident in dealing with the challenges of the last two years.'

It would be fair to say that the above tends to point towards success in both a conventional company and private life.

Comment: David Simmons

... it is common for organisations to want their senior managers to have a broader business perspective. But, frequently, managers have progressed through the managerial ranks because of their specialist or functional expertise. Suddenly, at least from the individual manager perspective, the goalposts and expectations shift. This is not always an explicit process.

It is interesting to note Rikki's emphasis on 'a way of thinking'. Peter Senge, in his book 'The Fifth Discipline', describes learning as 'a shift in thinking' – definitely the aim of the Thinking Organisation process.

The response rate to the follow-up questionnaire considerably exceeds expectations. The evaluations at the end of the programme and nearly two years on indicate that real personal change has occurred and I am delighted with the percentages still actively using the techniques.

The staying power of the Groundrules and the positive attitudes they have engendered at both a personal and professional level (and the complete lack of cynicism about them) are outcomes which many organisations who have produced 'values statements' would give their right arm for.

I continue to use MindMapping and Six Hats. Fellow participants on a course that I am attending have looked over my shoulder, seen my MindMapped notes and started to simply copy the style. I have run Six Hat sessions with course groups and, again, the response has been very positive during the session. Post course evaluations which encourage participants to reflect on learning, application and benefit reveal how much the technique has captured the imagination and been incorporated into participants' personal thinking style.

COMING UP-TO-DATE

The next group asked for comment are quite different. They are participants from the world of sport – Swindon Town Football Club, which is the first football club to accept that teaching thinking and actively creating the culture will improve the business. A cynic might point to my involvement with the Club and suggest a form of nepotism, but, as the saying goes, 'You can take a horse to water, but you can't make it drink'.

This group was newer to the process (six months), and their thoughts are relevant for two reasons:

1   They prove that you can get the playing side of sport to work closely with, and respect, the non-playing side's contribution.

2   The impact of the Thinking Organization is seen from Day One.

At this stage, seven people were directly involved (ultimately some 200 or so would be covered). They were, as you would expect, using the Groundrules and the thinking techniques.

THE QUESTIONS

1   How are you using the techniques?
2   Any other comments?

THE ANSWERS

Q.1   How are you using the techniques?

○   'Problem-solving, strategic planning, presentations.'
○   'Day-to-day affairs.'
○   'Prioritizing opportunities.'
○   'Assessing potential sponsorship opportunities.'
○   'Strategy, project planning, implementation – I used a combination of Mind Mapping, force field analysis, clustering and Six Hat Thinking.'
○   'Before beginning any major project I use force field analysis.'
○   'You can get round a problem and measure the result against the Groundrules.'

Q.2   Any other comments?

○   'I welcome the principle and it's not before time.'
○   'My previous company in no way encouraged staff to be creative or to look at developing performance. This major PLC is, I believe, representative of a good number of UK companies who make money in spite of themselves. Begs the question how much more could they make if they adopted the Thinking Organization concept.'
○   'Whilst the programme is still in its early stages, we are already seeing significant improvements in relationships between football and non-football activity. Generally good feedback from staff at all levels.'

And, just to complete the circle, as it were, here are some comments from those who have been taught by the participants:

○   'My boss seems more relaxed and prepared to listen.'
○   'Sounds exciting. I can't wait to get going.'
○   'I feel more secure because my boss is more relaxed.'
○   'I did something the other day I wouldn't have done if I had not heard of the Groundrules. I sold something – even though it is not my job. Before I would have told the customer to call back later.'

So there you have it. A programme based on a new concept, which **works at all levels**. That's the **view of the participants**.

For the record, some of the respondents were made redundant by me and were not terribly happy at the time. To read their positive comments, I suppose, proves that the Thinking Organization clearly shows everyone how they can benefit. It can move people above politics and has a way of drawing out the truth.

ACTION POINTS SUMMARY

CREATING THE ENVIRONMENT

1   **Vision:** Have you got one? Is it clear enough?

2   **Mission:** Have you got one? Is it a strategic statement – does it help your people make decisions about what they have to do to achieve your vision rather than just telling them what the company does?

3   **Groundrules:** Check self and company against these and think about the implementation process.

THINKING IN THE ENVIRONMENT

1   Look at how well you currently 'look after your brain' and plan how to fill any gaps in your maintenance programme. This could be helping the brain physically through working on the mind–body link, by mental challenge, mental stimulus and so on.

2   Analyse the 'thinking'/'doing' ratios in your company and plan how to get to the target ratios for yourself, your Senior Executives and your team.

3   Pick two or three techniques and have a go. Use simple problems at first.

LEADING IN THE ENVIRONMENT

1   Assess yourself against the leadership chapter, including the powerbases.
2   Assess your company against the knowledge base.
3   Gather some information on how you are perceived and consider what to do about the differences in view.
4   Consider what **you** mean by change and plan how to make it a way of life.

FINAL REVIEW BY TONY BUZAN

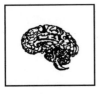 With results like those shown in Chapter 12, how can anyone fail to be convinced of the absolute necessity for implementing the ideas and approaches in this book? There is already an underlying trend towards the acceptance of the 'brain-based' economy. Here are some further examples showing how the movement towards the Thinking Organization is a rapidly growing one.

For 500 years companies have been valued, not as has been seen, by their book-recorded assets, but by 'goodwill' – a factor that may increase book value by as much as 20 times.

Sweden's financial services giant, Scandia, led by the inventor of the term and concept 'Intellectual Capital', Leif Edmundson, have blazed the trail encouraging companies to appoint 'Chief Knowledge Officers' (CKOs) and, already, a number of large multinationals have taken the advice: AT&T, Dow Chemicals, Monsanto, ICL, Glaxo and Wellcome.

The trend in which you are involved, by reading this book, is accelerating into a positive stampede. Consider the following:

○ Before 1990 international magazines were not using the brain as a front cover feature. Since that time, over 70 magazines have done so, the pattern being launched by *Fortune* magazine with its feature 'Brain Power', and continued by *Time, Newsweek, Scientific American, New Scientist, National Geographic, Life, Discover, Focus, Synapsia, South East Asian Economic Review, US News and World Report, Upbeat* and even *Biker* magazine! The brain and its future are becoming increasingly the vision of the planet.

○ In 1993 Scandia produced its first 'Intellectual Capital' supplement to its Annual Report. A large number of companies are following suit, and Scandia confidently predict that, by the year 2010, all company reports will be 'Intellectual Capital' reports with a standard financial supplement!

O   Mr Ton, the Prime Minister of Singapore, recently realigned his nation for global competition with the statement that Singapore would become known and successful worldwide under the banner 'Thinking Schools, Learning Society, Intelligent Island'.

O   The Brain Trust Charity recently declared the twenty-first century as the 'Century of the Brain' and the next millennium the 'Millennium of the Mind'.

In such a century, and in such a millennium, it is only Thinking Organizations that will survive.

This book has provided you with both the words and the theories to reinforce this message. It also gives you the practical means of achieving it in your own organization.

Use the Groundrules to create the correct cultural framework. Teach thinking techniques within that environment and, whether in business or at leisure, whether adult or child, you will create an enlightened, successful individual, company and planet.

You have already started to change by reading these pages; now all you have to do, as my good friend Rikki says, is 'go out there and ... do it!'

REFERENCES AND FURTHER READING

Buzan, Tony (1974), *Use Your Head*, London: BBC Books.

Buzan, Tony with Buzan, Barry (1993), *The Mind Map Book: Radiant Thinking*, London: BBC Books.

Buzan, Tony and Keene, Raymond (1994), *Buzan's Book of Genius*, London: Stanley Paul & Co.

Buzan, Tony and Keene, Raymond (1996), *The Age Heresy*, London: Egbury Press.

Covey, Stephen R. (1992), *Principle Centred Leadership*, USA: Covey Leadership Centre Inc.

de Bono, Edward (1990), *Six Thinking Hats*, Harmondsworth: Penguin Books.

Eales-White, Rupert (1994), *Creating Growth from Change: How you React, Develop and Grow*, London: McGraw-Hill.

Greenfield, Susan (1997), *The Human Brain*, London: Orion.

INDEX

Mind Skills for Managers

Samuel A Malone

How good are you at managing multiple tasks? What about problem solving and creativity? How quickly do you pick up new ideas and new skills?

Managers are measured against some tough criteria. You may feel that you're already doing everything that you can, and you're still being asked for more. But in one area you've got over 90% of unused capacity ... your brain.

Mind Skills for Managers will help you to harness your mind's unused capacity to:

• develop your ability to learn
• generate creative ideas
• handle information more effectively
• and tackle many of the key skills of management in new and imaginative ways.

Sam Malone mixes down-to-earth ideas with techniques such as checklists, step-by-step rules, acronyms and mnemonics to provide an entertaining, easy-to-use guide to improving your management techniques by unleashing the full power of your mind.

The skills in this book need to be practised. The best approach is to take one idea at a time and apply it. By following the book you will learn a whole range of 'mind skills' and be rewarded by measurable improvements in your performance.

Use and implement the ideas and you will think better, think faster and work smarter.

Gower

Gower Handbook of Management Skills

Third Edition

Edited by Dorothy M Stewart

'This is the book I wish I'd had in my desk drawer when I was first a manager. When you need the information, you'll find a chapter to help; no fancy models or useless theories. This is a practical book for real managers, aimed at helping you manage more effectively in the real world of business today. You'll find enough background information, but no overwhelming detail. This is material you can trust. It is tried and tested.'

So writes Dorothy Stewart, describing in the Preface the unifying theme behind the Third Edition of this bestselling *Handbook*. This puts at your disposal the expertise of 25 specialists, each a recognized authority in their particular field. Together, this adds up to an impressive 'one stop library' for the manager determined to make a mark.

Chapters are organized within three parts: Managing Yourself, Managing Other People, and Managing the Business. Part I deals with personal skills and includes chapters on self-development and information technology. Part II covers people skills such as listening, influencing and communication. Part III looks at finance, project management, decision-making, negotiating and creativity. A total of 12 chapters are completely new, and the rest have been rigorously updated to fully reflect the rapidly changing world in which we work.

Each chapter focuses on detailed practical guidance, and ends with a checklist of key points and suggestions for further reading.

Gower